Wall Between Worlds

WALL BETWEEN WORLDS
published by *Risen Angel Publishing*

Unless otherwise indicated, scripture quotations are from:
The Holy Bible, King James Version (KJV)

Information:
Risen Angel Publishing
British Columbia, Canada
risenangel@live.ca

I did not write it; I am merely the scribe who recorded it.
Another night; another dream: a day inside the night.

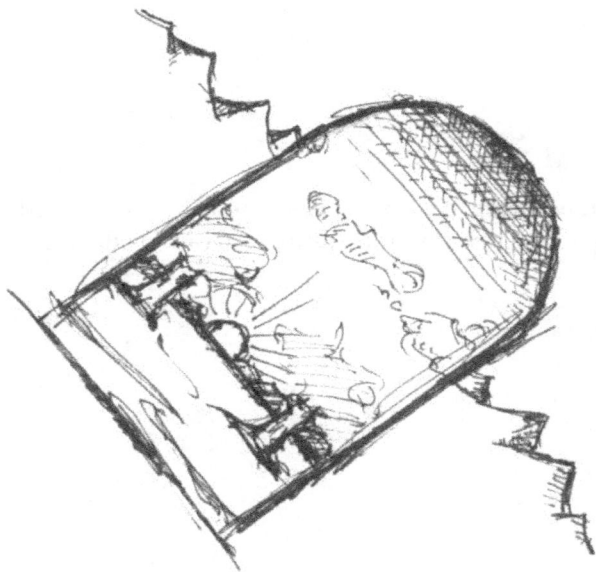

I wear a ring on this hand,
I found it in the sand.
It's a wedding band
Given to me by Christ,
So let me give you some advice:

Don't watch TV.
It's evil for you and me,
It's no mystery
Look at history –
Are you searching for victory?
Or just another fantasy?

I'll tell you what I see
When I turn on the TV…
Nothing that appeals to me.
I thought you wanted to be free
Or do you desire misery?

I want to be a light,
A soldier in the good fight;
I want to have God's sight,
And spread my wings in flight.
You ask if I have the right –

I tell you he is standing here,
He has never been so near;
Perfect love casting out fear,
Jesus shedding blood and tear.

So when the demons come in the night;
And I convulse with terror and fright,
Everything is going to be alright
Because he is here shining bright –
Like the morning star,
Not a shiny car.
You have fallen so far,
From where I come from.

Let me tell you about the Son
He is the only one,
That I want to know.

His seed I want to sow,
And watch the plant grow;
With faith – to faith,
From glory – to glory.

Understand?

Remember the band
I found in the sand?
It's on this hand,
Stretching across the land.

So raise your arms to heaven,
Stop tasting the leaven,
Because it's day seven,
It's hour eleven –

And the master is coming.

He is the one who has given
Me this house I live in,
All my sins forgiven,
And I want to know him.

He laid down his life
Set aside all strife, and
Took the church as wife.

Can I do anything?
He did everything.
What can I possibly do?
Look what he went through –

You look to the sky
And ask, why
Did he have to die?

David Burton

Because your sin is appalling,
And God is calling,
So stop falling,
  Into sin.

Let's begin
To live forgiven, and
Give hope to the hopeless,
  Faith to the faithless,
  A home to the homeless.

Do you have an ear
On the side of your head?
Then hear,
Before you're dead.

Because then it's too late.
You've become sealed to your fate,
And when you stand at the gate,
You will forget all your hate.

Clouds above;
Earth below,
Ask Jesus,
And know.

He holds the keys,
So fall on your knees,
And ask him, please –

What can I say,
How can I pray,
That you find the way,
Not tomorrow : today.

If you hear him clearly,
Do not harden your heart.
Stand against the fiery dart,
Because he loves you dearly.

Don't forget this rhyme,
Leaving it in due time;
Take it as a sign,
　　　　Not my will, Jesus, but Thine.

David Burton

TABLE OF CONTENTS

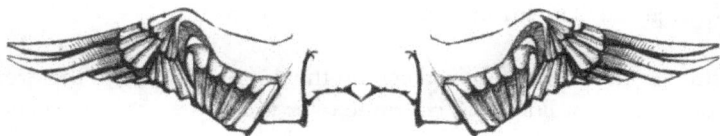

FOREWORD

I am a dreamer, a person who is able to remember their dreams with vivid detail. This book is a compilation of dreams, written with simple description, and left open to the interpretation of the reader. I form no hypothesis, draw no conclusion, and offer no explanation. The information stands on its own.

Through the years, I noticed certain themes developing in the dream sequences, plot lines that continue over the space of many years. I don't understand how this is possible, and I welcome you to investigate for yourself.

I have numbered the entries. Each number represents one night of dreaming. Often, I have multiple dreams in a single night. In order to distinguish between the dream sequences, I have added a keyword, **FLASH**, to help the reader. This keyword indicates I have transitioned from one dream into another, but have not awoken from sleep.

The entire book, from start to finish, was created by me; and every illustration was drawn by my hand.

One of the entries is not a dream, but an actual event. I have included it to demonstrate one important fact: the dreams are no longer bound to the spiritual realm, but have manifested in the physical.

David Burton

INTRODUCTION

I am sitting in the director's office with my head in my hands; the confusion, conflict and condemnation of the past several days has brought me here. I look up for a moment to glance at the painting on the wall and to look into his eyes.

"It's not working," I say. I turn my gaze once again to the floor and try to awkwardly express the concept within me.

"What's not working?" He asks.

"The power of the spirit."

"How do you know?" He catches me off guard; I didn't expect another question and I am answering it before I have a chance to think.

"I can't see it; I can't feel it; I can't hear it – "

"That doesn't mean it isn't working – what are you basing this on?" It's a leading question; he knows the answer: so do I.

"My senses."

We talk about many other things that are happening in my life, but this is the key concept. It is the primary object of my thought process that has essentially brought me to a halt. Nothing can progress beyond this until it is resolved. How do my dreams interact with this physical world? Is it instruction, prophecy, or both simultaneously? Why would he train me in the power and then forbid me to use it?

Leaving the director's office, I walk toward the blueberry field where I have been assigned to work for the day. It is not a glorious job to have, shoveling manure. However, it is not a leap for me. I usually work in the barn cleaning stalls.

The sun is shining and it is warm. I stand in the valley, looking at the mountains that surround me. I see rain clouds in the distance with rain bands beneath them. They are beautiful. I am thinking and talking about the ocean. My entire life was spent beside the sea, and it is a part of my soul.

For a moment I am left alone, considering everything that has transpired, years that have brought me to this field, at this moment. Without hesitation I raise my hand to the sky, palm outward, and use a part of me that I have left untouched for a long time – I *call*. I draw on the source, pulling it inside of me – and then send it, racing toward the clouds, exploding it in a shower upon impact.

Scripture is burning inside my mind, and I know exactly what I am doing. The anger and frustration of the past several weeks suddenly evaporates and I just let go: I can't take this anymore. I am what I am, not what these people want me to be. I basically just embrace myself as I raise both my hands to the sky and draw as deeply as I can. I feel it tingle in my body before I release skyward, pushing as hard as I can and bursting outward – I call the lightning.

I hear someone approaching; it is too late – they have seen me.

"It's going to rain," I say. He doesn't seem very interested. I look upward and discover why it suddenly appears darker. A storm cloud is directly above my head. I am surprised; that was extraordinarily quick. I don't know if this has happened before, and as the rain begins falling, I sense the response of a spirit stirring within me.

"What did you pray for?" I can sense the curiosity, but do not want to explain the method that I have chosen to communicate with God.

"Rain," I say quietly. The hail begins.

By the time we have reached the barn to put away our wheelbarrows and shovels, the first flash of lightning splashes across the sky directly above me and the thunder peals across the valley.

"More, Lord; more." I cry out. This is only going to escalate: I can feel it within me like a song being sung in my spirit. I am again left alone, and I stand still before the sky. I stare into the clouds and as the scripture plays across my thoughts, lightning fills the sky, stretching from one side of the clouds to the other.

Scripture appears inside my mind, blazing in white light. Words that speak of an angel, and watching the display in the sky above me gives me a new insight into the scripture. Right now I am in a conversation with God. So I fall upon what I know and start singing. I try to tell him how I feel through the words of song. I thank you, Lord. The storm grows with intensity; the rain falls from the sky in a torrential downpour, and white hail stings my skin. I am soaked; more water falls on me than does in the shower. I wring out my clothes.

As far as I know he has not responded this quickly or powerfully ever before in my life: while I was awake. He pours his answer out on me until I can take no more and I seek shelter. He sends the wind to drive the rain sideways: there is no escape.

I have not seen a lightning storm like this one in over ten years; it leaves a lasting impact on me.

I stand corrected: *the power **is** working, and I can see, feel, and hear it all around me.*

David Burton

15 In a dream, in a vision of
the night, when deep sleep
falleth upon men, in
slumberings upon the bed;

16 Then he openeth the ears of
men, and sealeth their
instruction,

17 That he may withdraw man
from his purpose, and hide
pride from man.

18 He keeps his soul from the
pit, and his life from perishing
by the sword.

Job 33

David Burton

PROLOGUE

I stand on a bridge with a river running rapidly beneath. In front of me stands the figure of a man made of darkness. It is a shadow. I instinctively know that I must cross the bridge.

Why? I don't know. It must simply be done. Turning back and walking away is not an option that is presented. I wrestle with the figure and both of us stumble over the edge of the bridge, plunging into the water below. I swim to the shore and climb out of the current. Something guides me as I begin to walk, and I am led to a cave.

There is a statue made of white stone in representation of an angelic creature. It has begun to crumble, but glows bright in the morning sun. There is a set of stairs leading into the tomb. I descend the flight quickly and find a group of people dressed in white, standing within. I speak to them quietly. I have become their leader now that the world has ended.

I lie to the people that stand in the coldness of the tomb. I twist their mind, destroy their life, and force them to witness their worst fear. I show them evil, and offer them a chance to become that evil. I tear away their innocence, and I feel good doing it.

CHAPTER ONE

I open my eyes.

I am staring out a glass window, and my gaze comes to rest on a mountain top a few miles away. Storm clouds surround the sky and darkness appears in the center. The clouds begin to swirl within the set boundaries of a triangle. The swirling mass of clouds within this focus suddenly darken. In the center of the triangle the clouds part, forming a circular opening.

The gateway is open.

A design is shown to me. I realize that is it important for me to remember it and I try to scrawl a sketch on some paper. I get the distinct impression that it will help me travel vast distances of space, maybe even time. The mountain top is magnified in my vision and I examine the device carefully.

The clouds form a tunnel of swirling liquid and I am deposited in another scene. I watch it recede and eventually disappear.

FLASH. There is a fight of ethics between myself and another who also witnessed this device. He has sold it to a company; somehow, I know this is not the intended use of the gift.

◆ **2** ◆

I am in a hallway. There is a door on my right. I open the door and enter the dark room. I feel a presence and know something lurks inside, hidden by the shadows.

"I know you are here." My eyes find the being and I look directly at it. The shadow phases into reality and moves hesitantly toward me.

"*You know.*" The voice comes from within my mind and it sparks no fear in me. I expected, I knew, I felt. I bare my forearm and the being injects me with a syringe.

David Burton

❧ 3 ❧

I am walking on a street, and there are houses on both sides. There are three women walking in front of me. I call to them and one turns around. There is a brief conversation.

Then a presence comes over her.

> "Bare yourself,
> shed a tear,
> and accept what you are."

One of the three chants several words and a green ball of fire leaves her hand, crashing into the roof of a house behind me.

FLASH. I am standing in a mountain range. There is snow and fields of ice. The three women are beside me. The same one speaks again.

> "Take this and protect it."

❧ 4 ❧

It is night. The moon is present. I am standing on a snow covered beach. I look out over the white ocean. I walk out to the edge and step onto the water. It is frozen. I feel shocked and confused. Why is the ocean frozen solid? I look to my left and am surprised by what meets my gaze.

A shining wall of opalescent color stretches out for miles in each direction, and reaches into the clouds above. I am drawn toward it, for I know something of its nature. I reach out and feel the surface of the wall. It is cold.

I pass through with ease and my eyes are presented with an interesting contrast. I am on the beach and the snow is gone. The ocean is calm and I can hear the waves gently crashing on the rocks.

A ways down the rocky sand I can feel the presence of people. I stroll quickly to where I am expected and enter an underground building.

These are my people, and they have been waiting. I am confused by what happens during the night; I awake.

The sun is shining and I can feel the earth below me, around me, inside me. I sense the approaching flood. I warn people and try to prepare them for what is to come.

> Some listen; some believe.
> Many will die.
> One door is safe; I ask them to seal the other.

FLASH. I am standing in front of a woman. She wears a face, not one I remember, but I know who she is. She is beautiful, sexy, seductress. I look into her eyes and know what she is thinking. I reach out and touch her. She is warm, soft and wet. I step back; she smiles.

"Come back. Meet me here, behind the wall." Turning away, she slowly walks toward *something* – I know what it is, yet I do not. I can't quite understand. I am not afraid; I am calm.

I am missing something.

～ 5 ～

I stand in a park. I walk upon green grass; a single tree stands a short distance away. A small figure stands near, her back turned to me. I notice her distinct female presence. She turns and stands up before me. She is dressed entirely in white. A hood surrounds her face, the only part of her body that is exposed with exception to her hands. Her eyes hold me spellbound: I can't look away. Her eyes I can see clearly, but the rest of her is blurred motion. Her eyes are rest.

I feel fear, terror, clarity.

David Burton

She looks into my soul and speaks. Her lips do not move, but her words echo inside my mind. She calls me by name; my Christian name.

"Risen, you are the one we have been looking for."

I desperately want to respond, but my body is paralyzed. I can't move; I can't speak. She knows I want to talk. The contact is ended. She awakens me from the dream, and my eyes open.

❦ 6 ❧

I am standing in a room, talking with a woman. Something distracts me, and I turn to my left. My eyes move toward that direction – an animal, sitting on a stool, is talking to me. It has her presence.

"Remember my words."

❦ 7 ❧

I am in an underground cavern. Bodies are scattered around, lying in decay. This place is full of disease.

FLASH. I am in a house. There is a crack in the ground, or floor. Black objects are oozing out. They are small cylinders. Virus, bacteria, unknown. I know they cause death. As I look on, more come out of the ground and I know: many will die.

I look at the scene. The black virus is lifting up from the ground and falling from the ceiling. It seems that there are two streams forming a wall. As I leave, a vision forms in my mind. I see a person reach into the wall. A black drop falls on his arm and his flesh is eaten away is if by acid. I return with a bottle of bleach and mist the wall.

Some die; some do not.

FLASH. I am looking at a shelf of plastic statues. I pull them down, separate them into the primary colors, and ball each pile of color into a sphere. I place the spheres on the table. I expect the watchers to be angry; instead, they are curious.

FLASH. I am standing in a devastated piece of earth. I am reminded of the aftermath of a nuclear blast, or plague. It seems as if I am standing in a crater, but I am not sure. There is only one man alive. He is working. I watch him for a second – he is piling bodies into a hole in the ground. I have the distinct impression of death.

I look to my left and see a woman. She is sitting on the ground, balled up, with her hands wrapped around her knees. She is sad, her face downcast, and her body ravaged by years of addiction. I approach her, crouch down, and look into her eyes. Reaching out my hand, I tuck her hair behind her ear and place my fingertips on the right side of her head.

"You can't see my hand, can you?" She pulls away slightly. Anger flashes across her face.

"No," she says calmly.

"What do you gain?" I ask her.

"Everything. Something you can't understand," she says as a presence comes over her. The pupil of her right eye dilates, turning entirely black.

I am filled with sorrow, despair. Slowly, I walk toward the edge. I am looking over the chaos – the death. I feel a hand on my back, I turn around. It is the man who was working. He grabs hold of me and holds me out over the edge. His face is filled with rage, and he is yelling.

"Give me three things to live for. I ask this of all before they take it. Tell me!"

I am frightened. I have a deep understanding of what he is saying. Somehow, I just know. I look at his eyes. I see the rage, anger and bitter sorrow. He likes the death and destruction no more than I.

"I want to live." My voice is calm, clear, powerful. He pulls me in, and sets me on the ground.

FLASH. I am on a cliff, overlooking the place where I was just standing. There is a screaming – in the throes of death. A huge pile of bodies lay below the edge I was held over. I see the man. He is pushing dirt over the pile of bodies with a machine. I hear the screams of the dying – they end abruptly as the dirt piles over them. I want to come down, but I do not know how. When the man is finished his work, he stands below me and looks up.

A thought enters my mind – *I have been shown.*

8

I am in a room and a woman stands in front of me – she is dressed in silky white. I know I can heal her pain. She removes her top, sliding the straps over her shoulders, allowing the nighty to fall to the floor. Her skin is a soft, creamy white color, and seems to glow freely. Her nipples are warm and hard; round and pink. Her breasts are firm and inviting.

She stands – confident and tall. No doubts cross her serene smile. She hooks her finger on the edge of her panties and slides them down her legs. She looks into my eyes and smiles. I am naked. We entwine together gracefully, softly brushing our skin. I run my fingers gently over her body, power flows from my hands, healing the wound in her soul.

FLASH. A clear night sky. I am in a clearing inside the forest. The stars shine bright in the black fabric sky. Something moves, and a light flashes. Looking up I see an object, hovering in the sky, defying the laws of physics. It spins like a quarter tossed into the air. It lands, and I enter.

That night, dreaming...
Of three cubes, with writing on their sides;
Of a bridge, separating two, holding one;
One of us was buried, if not all.
Of a war, which we were trying to stop;
A door, that only I could open;
Of the sea. They dropped four balls –
Killed everything within its waves, and shook the earth.
Behind the door was holy ground,
Not a place for fighting;
We came together in peace –
To save our lives, and the world.
It was gold – yellow, walls and floor.
They dropped four balls into the sea;
Tsunami waves.
We stood upon a rock;
The sea surrounded us – a wave approached.
It rolled – a craft appeared,
Opened its gate,
And saved our lives.

I am on a ship and we are flying above the treetops. I see the world slip away beneath me. There is a flash of blue light, and I find myself in a room, full of strange faces.

"I've only been gone two days," I say to them.

"How can you know this?" They ask.

FLASH. A woman approaches me and begins speaking clearly:

"There is something more than demons and angels and I believe you know." She is staring at me with intensity, her eyes penetrating into my soul. She turns and walks into another room – I follow. I sense that something is going to happen, and I can tell by her eyes that she already knows what it is.

David Burton

She is prepared for it, and spins quickly – she places her hand on me, increasing the connection between us (*mental, physical, emotional, spiritual*). She speaks, but her lips do not move.

"You will remember this as a dream, only a thousand times stronger." I sense the desperation inside her; she needs me to remember, for I am her only hope. She opens herself to me and images begin flashing inside my mind.

Suddenly, we are torn apart; an evil has come – we are connected to a system within a vessel, containing two chambers. She is on the right; I, on the left. For a moment, I am connected to the vessel, and I am overwhelmed by the technology. They begin a procedure on her as she screams silently.

Something snaps inside my mind and I break free, destroying the bindings that hold me paralyzed. I sense shock from our captors. They withdraw, as I remove her from the chamber. I lay her upon the floor – the embryo is coming; she may be dying.

She begs me to destroy it – she cannot, for she is weak. I place my hands on her, triangle formation, and call upon a power that is forgotten. It comes with fire – I pulse, releasing a white nuclear energy.

11

I asked for understanding; received an answer, and forgot. I am given a ring that interlocks with another. I am told, "Trust is not an option." And, I wake up, screaming.

12

Once they were pure, then something happened: a mutation, a communion between two souls. I believe they are dying, or the lightning brings tears.

❧ 13 ❧

The ocean plays at my feet, and if I focus my energy it moves for me. I can live within the waters, and see the light dance across the sky, reflected on the surface of the sea above me.

❧ 14 ❧

Three lives I live while asleep this night. Each is a powerful, waking vision.

THE FIRST

The heroin comes from the needle I have pressed against my arm. I feel the prick as it slides under my skin and the rush as it enters my soul. Naked, dirty, sick – I lay, leaning against a wall in a city somewhere. I know this goes on for an eternity, day after miserable day – craving, searching, fixing. Anxiety and panic grip my throat. I need, trapped in a constant drive; a terrible, yet irresistible force that awakens within.

THE SECOND

A girl whose skin is soft and flesh is young. I seek her because she frees me. Sexual desire captures my mind in an illusion of bliss – she is the sweet warmth I have pressed against my skin. She is the needle I have pressed against my arm.

THE THIRD

There is a war being fought all around me as I run through a field of golden wheat. I have left the group behind me, and run through the woods – I seek escape; a release from this torture and monotony of war. An oblivion hidden in a mountain side.

❧ 15 ❧

As I lay my head down on my pillow, I felt a presence in my room. Ignoring it as I had the many nights before, I closed my eyes and waited for sleep. Soon, the darkness surrounded me, and fear followed. The presence had a voice and it spoke to me directly.

The dream began:

A woman approaches me on a stairway. She carries a blade in her left hand. Her eyes are wild, but her manner calm. She strikes at me with the blade, but I stop it with my right hand. I feel the cold steel pierce my skin, but the wound does not bleed. I take the blade in my fingers and turn it.

She releases the blade and walks away. I follow her, entering a house covered in darkness with a dim light burning within. Inside I find a man that has gone insane. I recognize him from somewhere, and I know I have spoken to him before.

For some reason I lay down to sleep; to dream – and within this dream: I dream. The torture begins anew, with a vengeance and force that I have not known prior. I am in torment.

"You can't withhold yourself from me for I know your fear," says a dark presence standing beside me. I am writing words upon a page and the presence is enraged. It comes near to me, demanding:

"Submit, or I will take you, and destroy you."

Darkness crashes down upon me, as figures blur, encircling me. I am lashing out in any direction while screaming my defiance. I move quickly, blur, attack. I dance the dance of death.

"Betray your God."

I am shown the writing again. This time, words are in bold face and the presence touches them. Words stand out as if on fire. They mean something important, and I have written them. The presence wants them destroyed – he does not want others to see; to know.

"Destroy it."

I refuse. Alone and terrified, I stand against the darkness.

Wall Between Worlds

FLASH. I hover in the air, throwing blades – they fly fast, spinning through the night air, hitting the target: another figure hovering, doing battle with me. The blade sinks in, multiplies and splits the demon's body in half – exploding outward.

FLASH. I am in the room again with the dark presence standing beside me. There is a dim light burning inside the room.

We, once more, stand before the writing. I am exhausted, beaten, and tortured. I try to commit the message to memory. I almost grasp it. My time is near, at an end. I reach out, quickly running my fingers over the words; they turn color and the color spreads rapidly, coating the entire text.

The presence screams and casts me down. I struggle to wake; but, can't – forced to stay in this nightmare. I am not sure if I destroyed the words, but it got what it wanted and let me out of the dream.

I awake on my bed, opening my eyes and trying to grasp my surroundings. I am searching for evidence that I am finally out of the dream for real. I feel relief as I search the room – it looks normal. I begin to put on my shoes, but the world begins to fade as I tie the laces.
I awake on my bed, opening my eyes. There is the sound of someone knocking on my door, and a voice echoes inside my mind:

"I am knocking at your door."

Finally, I awake for the last time.

❧ 16 ☙

The Heavenly Army Sails.

❧ 17 ☙

Jesus Christ, please save me. Take me from this earth and allow me to see the eyes of angels – bring me into the place of white light, and show me what I have forgotten. Teach me the ways that have been left behind, locked away behind the doors of thought. Amen.

David Burton

❦ 18 ❧

In this country, the financial institutions charge people money for not having any, churches are alarmed, and war is waged for oil.

❦ 19 ❧

I stand in a dimly lit room. I sense that it is underground. The walls are made of old red brick and the mortar is dry and crumbling. There is a window on one side of the room and behind the window sits a man who distributes mail to the appropriate people.

At first, I appear to be alone, but I soon understand that there is another man present in the room. He is just beyond the edge of my peripheral vision, but his voice rings clear in the abandoned shelter. He is teaching me how to move objects with my mind. I am fascinated by what he speaks and even more so by the result of his teaching.

I am given three objects to play with: the first I throw against a wall and just before it reaches the peak in its arc, I call it back and it comes flying through the air into my outstretched hand. I am amazed. I try again with another object, but it falls to the ground and refuses to respond to my call. I turn to my teacher, but he avoids my gaze and says, try again: this time it works. I begin to understand that it is simply *faith* that enables me to call the object. With even the slightest amount of doubt the object will not respond to my call.

I exit the building and enter the cold cobble street. There are buildings lining the pathway, each of various height and design. The second lesson begins and I am taught how to lift myself from the ground with the use of sheer will. Again, without faith, I remain bound to the earth or fall mid-stream. I convince my mind of the truth of this teaching and begin to acquire the objects set at the peak of each building.

I lift myself from the ground and move quickly toward the final ledge but do not make it on my first attempt. My thoughts fail me. I allow myself to believe that the ledge is just a little too far out of reach, or that my ability does not allow me to attain a certain height.

The one who teaches me has no physical form, having discarded it before entering the pathway, yet his voice enters into my mind. I sense his anger at my disbelief and I am disciplined for my failure. I try again. This time I am determined to achieve what I seek and do not allow the weakness of my mind to interfere. I land swiftly on the highest ledge. The next lesson begins.

This lesson is the final one before I am set free to play with the newly bestowed knowledge. It is a lesson of destruction. The one who is teaching me brings me once more into the dimly lit room. He quickly explains the process by which such destruction is called and unleashed upon the physical world. I listen intently and in confidence. His speech ends quickly after pointing out a few key pieces of knowledge. I am allowed to use all that has been taught me to destroy the earth. I am freed.

I try to warn the people in the building. In fact, I specifically go out of my way to talk to each one before I leave the room. I tell them of the eminent destruction and give reason for them to leave the place where they are. I speak clearly so they will understand the seriousness of my words and take quick action. I walk outside the room and wait until they come outside. One refuses to stay out, and returns to their home inside.

It can't be helped: I am committed to my path and have been shown what I must do. In a sense, I have no choice but to continue. I reach out with my mind and destroy the building in a fury. I watch as it comes collapsing down, hidden in a blanket of gray cloud. I feel sadness for the loss of life, but harden my heart against it.

My teacher is gone and I stand quietly in the street. My words have sparked a following, and a series of events unfolds rapidly in the time continuum of space within my mind. I witness future events and walk through the doorways of a thousand worlds. I watch the people that come to believe in what I have done and begin to follow. In the space of a moment I have lived an eternity of happenings.
My mind returns to the present, and I begin the fight.

⁓ **20** ⤔

I am in a distant city. I am walking with a woman, approaching a house I've never seen before. We enter through the door and come to stand in the living room. There is a man sitting on the couch, and an evil presence hovers inside him. I sit on one side of the man, and the woman sits on the other. I try to talk to her, but she refuses to respond. I leave for a moment, and when I return, her body lay on the floor, broken, bruised and destroyed – the light is gone from her eyes.

FLASH. I know that they are coming. I have a prophecy that speaks of these events and I am prepared. There is a needle destined for my arm. They kill the others around me. The attacker takes his shoes off, and I steal them, placing them on my own feet. I turn the table of events and flee.

FLASH. I find her quickly because she is waiting for me. We come together and fall into an embrace. I wrap my arms around her and press my lips against hers. The kiss is sweet and the tingling sensation within my lips sends a pulse throughout my entire body. I want her, with no questions; I want to rip her clothes off – then she looks into my eyes and *damn* – she is gone.

Surrounded by darkness, I search for some visual hold: some reality to remind me that I do indeed exist, and that only a moment before, stood in the presence of the most angelic creature I have ever seen. I call for her. I call for escape, and peace descends within me.

A holographic image comes to life in front of my eyes, and I find myself once more staring at the girl – although this time she has no life – she is only an image, a mere shadow of her former self, retaining her natural beauty, but not her spirit. No soul is found inside the image presented to my eyes.

But I know that beyond the image lay reality, and the soul; so I reach out and break the barrier.

❦ **21** ❧

I stand on the side of an embankment, looking out over the ocean. The water is blue with an intensity unseen by mortal eyes. The waves move with motion defying the laws of gravity. The sand slips away under my feet, cascading down upon the driftwood marked pathways. A scream echoes over the stillness of the scene.

The water comes alive, and I respond to its call. I stretch forth my arms and cry out the words that will calm the water. Fabric flying around my presence is whipped into shape by the wind coming off the water. My vision is clear. The thoughts within my mind are focused. There is no way to penetrate the trance I have placed myself into for this brief period of time.

I am speaking to the water. "Come," I say. She ascends and walks out into the storm driven sea. The storm is that of our minds crashing together in a communication that has been long overdue – communion of our essence as we touch each other gently. The power of our minds is raw and each with caution allows play of fingertips on the wind. Neutrality remains streaming in the air and is driven by the force of the wind. There is no breeze here.

I see her standing in the center of the sea with an old woman at her side. I can hear the old one advising her to remain. "Do not venture upon the wind," she emphasizes to her young one. The young girl silences her with a gesture and flashing eyes. Words have been spoken but I have been denied access to their exchange. It doesn't matter. Her attention is on me now. Her eyes are a crystalic blue matching the spectrum of the waves that surround and obey her voice.

She walks to the edge of the dark sandstone but pauses as she reaches the water. The sea laps gently at her feet, but waves stretch back from the stone, viciously curving upward into the gray sky. She is the pivotal point in a universe made of hydrogen and oxygen, combined in the essence of life. In this place, she rules over her subject with grace and gives screaming words to what the water can't voice.

David Burton

Our eyes are locked in gaze while our minds entwine within the seascape. We are dancing on the wind; I feel her within me – I am within her. We stare back at ourselves from each other's eyes. It is a sharing of which has no beginning and no end. This is the image of our love, although we can't explain or acknowledge it yet. Living in such loneliness craving passion and unable to find what we long for in each independent world.

She steps out upon the water; I step out upon the air. With a thought I send her cloak blowing backward snapping in the wind; with a laugh I feel the rain drops pelting against my face. We are dancing.

I watch as she moves her fingers and sends waves cresting up into the air. She stands upon the water, using it as a platform. Her elegant beauty is raw and pure, a reflection of the ballet driven seas.

The water is, by extension, the face of her mood; an expression that can't be worn by her commanding presence. To watch her without seeing the infinite flow of her ocean is to eat the stem of an apple and toss the fruit to the ground. I close my eyes and beckon the wind to come close. Catching the essence of what I am, I move across the surface of her skin; falling into the valley before riding upward and flying from the wave crest.

I am a fleeting breeze blowing across the water. I am known even as I know her. There is no doubt, she can feel my touch. We must make quite a scene – she standing upon her wave, and I suspended in the wind.

22

I stand in an underground cavern. The water laps against the rock shoreline and the moss covered walls seem to illuminate the small area. There is a barrier wall directly in front of me. It appears to be made of water, suspended in the air, causing the image of the world beyond it to be distorted. There are two angels in human form standing across from me, their wings are folded and hidden beneath their robes. One is covered in white cloth and the other wears gray. It is the gray that speaks first.

"This is *other*," says the voice.

"I know," spoken quickly and without thought, "I've been here before."

"Your eighth wing is in danger," echoing in my ears, "they will try to take it." I am confused. I hear the words but they make no sense. I can't understand the message.

"Eighth wing?" I ask. The gray has little patience and becomes frustrated with my lack of comprehension. This sparks motion in the one dressed in white and wearing the face of a man. As he walks past he gestures at the gray to be still. He walks calmly toward me and places his hand on my chest.

"Here," speaks the voice clear inside my mind. It is different than the first. I gain understanding, but it is only of something still to come. I feel confident that the one in white has relayed a message, but what it contains still puzzles me. It is as if a seed has been planted inside my mind and within the seed are the words. In time all will be revealed. I sense relief but I can't distinguish between the three emotional presences in the cavern. All minds have become, in some way, shared. It is through this partial joining that I am reassured all will be well in time. I need only have patience.

I sleep.

For God, who commanded
the light to shine out of
darkness, hath shined in our
hearts, to give the light of the
knowledge of the glory of God
in the face of Jesus Christ.

2 Corinthians 4:6

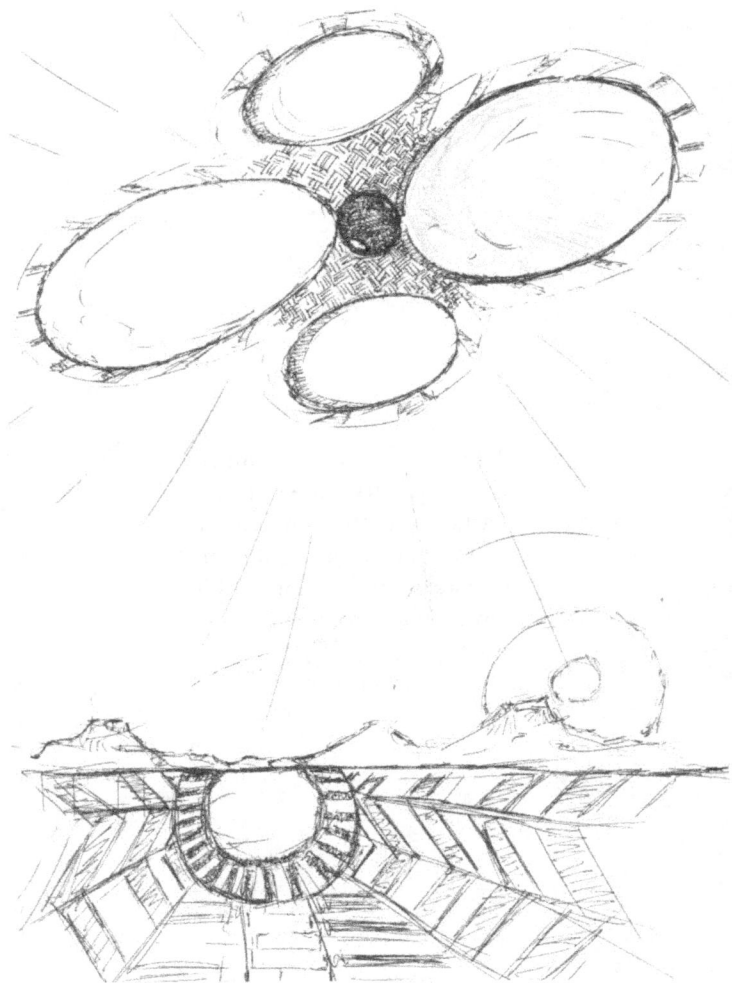

David Burton

CHAPTER TWO

My eyes are aching and my body is sore; each day is filled with pain, inflicted by my own hands. I sit now in the chapel and will soon close my eyes – the time is upon me.

I could not enter the dream world on my first try; blue light surrounded me, but I could go no further. I shifted position and away I went. The blue light brought back memories of last night's journey, and the lands I travelled. I remember a woman trying to restrict my access, and trying to keep me blind, but I broke free and walked the world.

At one point we become involved in a discussion. She is projecting disappointment. I say, "What do you want from me? That I call my angels?" She immediately perks up, her eyes lighting, excitement brimming. "Not those angels," I say coldly as I turn and walk away.

FLASH. I feel out of place, unwanted and unnoticed; people are shunning me. I am in a house and the woman in the house is having a stairway replaced. I walk the stairway once, venturing downstairs. When I return, the stairway has been removed. The vacant space is covered and framed. A new floor is standing in its place. After removing my shoes, I walk out onto the floor, and find the structure weak.

"I am going to shatter this floor," I say to the constructor beside me. "I can feel it giving away." I feel embarrassed that I have put such pressure upon the structure. "Support must be added," I say, projecting the image of how it can be done.

✎ **2** ✎

I awaken in another world. I am standing on a mountain, and the devastation is apparent all around me – a war has taken place or is still being fought. I take a vehicle and flee. I have a vague memory of being pursued.

FLASH. I am standing in a meeting of the remaining forces. We are what is left of our kind – our soldiers, warriors, fighters. Many people look to me for guidance and leadership. Many others look to another man. There is a battle ensuing between these two factions of people, and war is about to break out amongst us. I have an idea of how to bring us together. I walk over to the man and say, "There is a way to stop this. I give it all to you."

What the two factions fight for I unite under one man. He is shocked, and asks me to verify. I can see in his eyes that he understands what I am saying and doing. His eyes thank me, while asking, "Are you sure?"

"Yes," I reply silently.

"So be it." Our unspoken exchange ends and I turn to leave, knowing the pathway has been embarked upon. As I am turning to walk away, a man comes from my peripheral, grabs his head, pulls it back, puts a gun beneath his chin and simultaneously pulls the trigger three times while slamming his head into the concrete.

"No!" I scream, running toward him. My scream and my journey to reach him is an eternity. I am having my heart torn out again just writing this down. Tears stain the page.

FLASH. I am in a house far away from the war. I have been brought here by my family, for some purpose I am unaware of. I am guided by an unseen hand. I feel protected, yet totally disconnected from my family.

I am an alien amongst these people. I go to the girl's room who lives in this house, a girl whom I have loved for a long time. I have been gone for so long now that I am afraid she will reject me, or have fallen away. As I wait for her to arrive I experience these feelings but when she walks inside my love for her awakens once again, and it is powerful. She is shocked to see me – I see it in her eyes. I also see the love although she hides it.

I do not understand.

David Burton

The evening is a series of events that escalates to me having bitter words with her guardian. I am sorely unimpressed by his actions. Had I not come from such a sickening and painful place just prior, I would have surely killed the man.

3

I wake in a world far away, where a storm is raging and all the ships are coming into harbour. I see signal fires on an Island, but no one is stopping to help them. I love the people on the Island. I look at the clouds and know the storm will soon hit.

I take a wooden boat and two ancient oars, running into the water to begin my crossing. Nothing stands in my way, and I will allow nothing to. My ship is destroyed; yet, I swim. I reach the Island and return, but what transpired in between is lost to me now.

Perhaps one day I will return, and I will save those I love; carry them across the sea, and bring them into my arms.

4

Demons keep coming to me and asking, "Where is Risen? We are searching for him." None are able to recognize me until I reveal myself and fight. I tell them, "Until you go out and use for seven years, don't speak to me." I take away their power.

5

I am on a ferry, crossing from one ocean to another. On the vessel there is drinking, gambling and destruction. People lose everything they have – people swear it off, never wanting to touch it again. I am the owner of the vessel, but someone else has taken control, and is piloting the ship.

I go below deck, into the heart of the machine, searching for something. The inside is immense – the physical space is larger than the vessel itself. Here I encounter the most beautiful blonde woman I have ever seen. We fight against each other, but our struggle ends with her straddling me. I am trying to slide into her.

"You're not wet," I say.

"Well, it's not like you tried very hard," she replies.

❧ **6** ☙

I awake in the country side. I am standing in a field, looking a group of houses that form a small community. I see a young girl, but no one else. The girl explains to me that the village is very poor, and is made up of invisible people. I can't see anyone, but I hear the voices of other women. I have the impression that I have stumbled across the village of a sorceress.

An old iron railway passes through the village, and enters a cave just outside the border of the community. Inside the cave is an ancient platform, acting as a station, and the railway goes no further. As we walk toward the cave, I see the train arrive, but before we reach the platform, it disembarks, and I am stranded.

I ask my guide when, and if, the train will return. She assures me that it will, but I have my doubts.

❧ **7** ☙

I am standing on the shore as a ship arrives, watching the people come off the boat. I am waiting for someone who does not arrive. I walk down the road, knowing that she is coming. I see her approaching from a distance. I sense it is her, but when she nears me I see that she has aged – she looks a thousand years older – her skin is changed, her hair is white, and her eyes are on fire with blue light.

She walks by me. I stand still for a minute as she continues walking. I am trying to understand. Suddenly I have clarity. I run to her and say, "I didn't think you'd come." There is a shimmer and she looks young again.

A spell is cast; a spell is broken.

8

"You think I can't leave my body and walk, a thousand miles away?" I ask, and silence them all.

9

The time of decision is upon me. I have come to a place in my journey where I must forsake everyone and everything I ever knew, or stay imprisoned forever. My mind is made up. I remove my clothes, enter a pool of water, and submerge myself completely. This is my act of change.

After dressing in new clothes, I search for the woman who is ever-present with me. A woman so beautiful, that tears form in my eyes when I think about her. A portal opens in the air beside me, and she appears at my side. She begins to talk of mundane things, not understanding that something has changed within me. My mind is already reaching into a future that she can't see or understand. I tell her I am leaving. I must. I have unfinished matters which need to be attended to.

"I am leaving tomorrow," I say. She tries to hold on to the world she knows and understands. I look into her eyes, and see the pain of rejection. She interprets my leaving as betrayal. Anxiety rises within me. I don't want to lose her, but I know I will if I don't take a risk, and show her my heart.

The rain is falling around us. As she turns to walk away, across the rain soaked dirt, I reach out to her. I wrap my arms around her, and pull her tight against my body. She struggles briefly, and then holds me tightly. We are in love (*combined and unbroken – it has always been this way; and, thus it will ever be*).

"I am leaving," I whisper in her ear.

"No," she says. "Please stay." Her eyes plead with me, evoking sadness.

"And if I do?" I ask hesitantly. "Will you forsake everything to be with me completely?"

I ask for her love, and give mine in return. We are interwoven, imprinted, and intimately known. There is an exchange of words between us, and the promise of a future. She turns, walks through the portal, and disappears.

I turn my attention to the world around me.

I am standing in a city, near a building, with a vacant phone booth nearby. As I walk toward the telephone, a car appears out of the darkness. There are three men inside the vehicle, and a white decal of words on the glass windshield. The car stops, a door opens, and a man steps out.

A vision unfolds inside my mind, and I see the events before they happen. I know this man is here to kill me, and I know the weapon he will use. I KNOW. The world suddenly slows. I begin to take another step, but time appears to have nearly stopped. I see the man coming around the side of the vehicle, weapon drawn.

He begins firing the instant he is clear of the obstruction. I feel the bullets enter my body, piercing my skin. Several enter my chest, my side, my torso, and my legs. The man pauses, assuming that this is sufficient. He is wrong. My foot finds the surface of the pavement, my step complete, and I am still standing.

Irritation surfaces upon his face as he raises his gun higher, solidifies, and fires several more rounds into my head. I feel [see; experience; flow with] the bullets enter my mind. I feel the blood coming from these wounds [virus; doubts]. I feel the pain of this vicious attack, and watch as he crawls directly up a vertical wall, perching on the edge of the building, attempting to verify his kill.

I refuse to accept the pain. I walk toward the phone, taking several steps of sheer agony, held up only by my faith. I pick up the phone, and begin dialing. The demon watches from his perch, shock rippling across his face. I am bleeding, but fully engaged in the battle. The phone line connects.

David Burton

"I need help," I say into the receiver.

The demon screams a shrill wail, and fires several rounds into my face. Time resumes its normal pace. I've had enough, and I embrace the anger now burning inside of me. I approach the demon with violence. I call on the power, speak the words, and *cast* with rage in my heart. My words run deep.

The demon is annihilated, but the fire within is still burning. I turn away from the destruction, and notice that two men have appeared a short distance away. They are looking at me intently. I am bleeding, but won't let them near me because I assume they are here to finish the job the last creature started. As my anger fades, I recognize the truth and assurance they are projecting, and I allow them to help me.

"All is changed now; you have become aware — we must leave."

As I explain my wounds to them, a blue light [*shield*] surrounds me. I think my wounds are severe, but they assure me it is not so. As they continue speaking to me, I realize the bleeding has stopped, and the wounds are healed. The only pain I feel is the bruising of the projectiles.

"You've only broken a small amount of shielding in one area," they say, or something similar. They open a gateway in front of my eyes and we all enter, wearing the blue shields. I know nothing will ever be the same again and I look at the people as we walk. I begin to cry.

"I need a wizard," I say.

"*You* just might get one," they reply – sincerely.

∾ 10 ∾

It is night. I am standing in a clearing, hidden inside a white cloud, staring at the trees before me. There is a pathway leading into the forest. Several women gather around me, and my father is at my side. He turns, and looks me in the eye.

"Look at the sky," he says. I turn my head, looking down the pathway through the trees, where he is drawing my attention.

I see a light, exploding across the sky, like starlight only a thousand times more intense. It is daylight. With the explosion I kneel in the white sand beneath my feet, and look to the sky. Darkness falls immediately.

A woman beside me puts her arm around me. I feel violated. "You should not be on your knees," she says. "You should sit like the rest of us."

I stand, rising with fury in my heart.

"NEVER," I scream, mentally and verbally – piercing the darkness and shattering the vail. Turning away from the woman, I walk down the path, passing my father along the way. "I am leaving," I say.

My father rises to follow. I open a gateway, a portal inside the dream world, which acts as a doorway from one place to another. I walk through the portal, my father follows, and we find ourselves standing in front of a building.

"What is this fury inside of you?" He asks.

"It is dark," I say. "It can't be dark. It is early." The gateway is still open behind us. I draw his attention to it. I point to the sky within the gate, and then the sky outside the building.

One sky is light; the other is dark. "I must go *now*," I say and race toward the gate. I leave my father, and return to the white sand.

꽁 11 ꙮ

I come across an insanely high wall that is built between two mountains. I ascend, standing upon the wall, and all that remains within me.

David Burton

12

I am in a prison of genetics. They have begun the study of demonology in the physical realm. In other words, the demons are breeding [*reproducing; being created*].

13

I learn how to draw mountains, and many gates with flowers.

14

I'm standing outside a building, waiting for a man to bring me cocaine. I try to follow him inside, but I am not allowed. I wait. He returns shortly with an ounce of cocaine. I take the white powder, and deliver it to a woman. I take a percentage of the powder, but I want more.

Addiction takes me by the throat, metaphorically, and I start fighting within myself. The cocaine spills all over me, and powder blows everywhere.

15

It's payday. I take my cheque to the bank, and cash it, placing all the cash inside an envelope. I return to my house, walk up a flight of stairs, and go to sleep. I awake and leave my house but someone is sleeping in the hallway outside my door. I give him the keys to my house and leave.

16

I am on a lost Island with a group of people. We are taking raw glass, polishing it, and cutting it into half cubes. Some of us do not want to be a part of this anymore. We have come to realize that the crystal we create is fake, and the man we work for is an asshole.

17

I am in a field, walking toward several houses. I can sense her, the woman I love with the very depth of my soul. She is near. I can see her, standing on the peak of a house. I call on the power, lift myself from the ground, and land on the roof top. I close the distance between us, and we talk quietly for some time.

"They are coming for me," she says. "I'm scared."

"Don't be afraid. I will fight them, and I will not lose."

Suddenly, they appear. As they race toward us, I send her to hide. I summon blades into my hands, throwing knives. I send them spinning through the air, willing them to hit their target, and draw blood. The blades find their destination, slicing my enemy. They fire rounds of ammunition at me, piercing my skin. However, I am aware of this tactic, and the bullets do no damage. I fight, fly, and search for her.

FLASH. I stand upon a mountainside, near a building. I enter the building, and ascend to the second floor. I walk into a room filled with people. We are discussing the displacement of objects. Our discourse finishes, and we ascend to the next level of the building. There is a doorway I want to walk through, but it is guarded by evil. Here, an evil presence takes the people away from me. In frustration, I leave, once more returning to the ground.

My loss of belief lasts only for a moment. I remember my ability, and lift myself into the air. I ascend the stairway, destroy the presence, and enter the doorway that was before closed to me.

Behind the door, I find many people gathered for a meeting. Not many are aware of my presence. I walk among the people, looking into each person's eyes, scanning the room. Each person's eyes have a different level of light – some glow brightly; others, weakly. I do a double take at one glance, seeing a face that is a shadow, with no eyes emerging.

"Where am I?"

❧ 18 ❧

I am in my room, laying on my bed, trying to enter my body, but I can't – something is inhibiting the transfer. I can see my body; I can feel my body – but I can't activate it. I am being held captive by an evil force. I forget the words that will free me from this nightmare.

I awake within the dream, rise from my bed, and descend the nearby stairway. Someone is standing near the landing, and I begin to tell them about my dream. The world fades around me and,

I awake within the dream, rise from my bed, and descend the nearby stairway. I see a woman standing near the landing. The walls of the stairwell are dripping with blood. The world fades around me and,

I am in my room, laying on my bed, trying to enter my body, but I can't – something is inhibiting the transfer. I can see my body; I can feel my body – but I can't activate it. I stop trying to enter my flesh, and embrace the spiritual. I turn away from my body, *raging*, but this time I close my eyes, and fight the demon that is trying to bind me. "I don't care how many times I have to awake and descend these stairs," I scream, "I WILL NOT BETRAY!"

I descend the stairs, while simultaneously fighting to enter my body. I have remembered the words that will set my free from this darkness, but my voice is taken from me. I panic, I struggle, there is pain in my neck, a spasm – I fight, now knowing I could remain in this torment for a very, very long time.

"Je – Jes – Jesu – Jesus Christ our Lord – In the name of – I CAST THEE OUT, YOU FUCK!" I awake, screaming the words into the emptiness of my room.

❧ 19 ❧

I am standing in an old abandoned house. The lock on the door has been broken, and someone else holds the key. The place is a disaster. It's flooded, the water is stagnant, and algae is growing on its surface. A man stands inside the room. I demand the key, but he refuses to return it. In the center of the room there is a pool, filled with naked women. I approach the edge of the pool, and reach for one of them.

"So, you choose her," a woman's voice intones. She appears out of nowhere, and looks at me appraisingly. "She is already taken."

"I don't care," I say. "I've fallen in love with her. If you stand between us, I will go to war." True to my words, the world attempts to separate us, and I fight against every force that rises against us.

The dream ends with us standing on a battlefield, our hands linked together, our souls interwoven.

20

I am standing in a world, far away. There is a hole in the earth in front of me. It appears to be excavated, and a strange metal encases the expanse. Inside the hole there is a bowl, filled with spheres. The spheres are laying scattered inside the bowl, motionless. I intrinsically understand the technology, and know that these spheres are supposed to be hovering inside the bowl, cycling the neutrons of an atom. This is supposed to operate on its own; however, it is broken – so, I fall into the hole, and activate the machine. The spheres rise and move chaotically around within the confines of a larger, invisible sphere. I have an understanding which lose upon waking.

If we live in the Spirit, let us
also walk in the Spirit.

Galatians 5:25

David Burton

CHAPTER THREE

I decide to walk aboard a sea vessel [*a ship; a boat; a craft*]. I sit down at a table and listen as the female guitarist plays a song. I decide to consume alcohol, as others are indulging and it is offered to me.

As soon as I allow the drink within my body I black out, and awake standing on a distant shore of a foreign land. I watch in shock as the ship I had been on drifts past, entering a secure area. I run, chasing after it; I hope to find a way back on board. I encounter a guard who leads me to another table, where I explain my situation.

The guard informs me that I must complete certain documents before I will be allowed to board the ship. I quickly agree, and as I sign the papers my fellow travelers arrive. I place the pen on the table and run toward them. The guard tells them to fill out different paperwork.

I say that I will write mine the same as theirs; the same documents. As soon as I move to do this the guard tenses and nearly draws his weapon. I ask to join my fellow travelers and fill out the same paperwork as they.

One man, sitting – with glowing blue green eyes – speaks to me without hesitation.

"No. You must do it *our* way." He shows me mentally that I can join my acquaintances; however, I must abide by his rule and write the documents he gives me, not those of the other people.

I concede, join the female guitarist, speak and awake.

❧ 2 ❧

I'm at work, living in a foreign city. I finish my shift, and cash my cheque. I walk home quickly, open the door and stare at my empty apartment. There is a restlessness within me. I haven't been using lately, but tonight I want cocaine. I place a call to my dealer.

"I need an eight ball," I say impatiently. "How long?"

"I don't have it," she says. "I need to make a call."

"No," I reply quickly. "I need it now. Make it happen, or someone else will." I hang up the phone, and wait for the dealer to arrive. She soon appears, and I walk outside to meet her. I give the cash.

"I don't have it on me," she says. "I need to go pick it up."

My anger and frustration begin to swirl within me as I watch her walk away with my money. I can't believe it. I never should have given her the cash without seeing the product first, but my impatience has once again ruled my decisions. Time passes, but she does not return. I call her again.

"How long?" I ask.

"I don't have it," she says. "It might take until tomorrow."

I slam the phone down into the cradle, and berate myself for my stupidity. How many times? How many times does this have to happen before I learn? As I begin raging, my sister shows up at my door with a man I've never met before. I've always hidden everything from my family, but I am in desperate need.

"Can you get me anything?" I ask the man.

"Yes," he says. "Come with me."

FLASH. We are standing inside a room, having acquired the cocaine I need. He pulls the bag out of his pocket, and then hides it from me. I start losing my mind.

"What are you doing?" I say, "All this talk of acceptance, and such, but you don't want to see me use!?" I take the drug from his hand, tear it open, and load my pipe. My hands are shaking; cocaine falls to the floor. My sister leaves crying, the man leaves, and I am alone.

I smoke, confused as to why these people left. I hear my sister crying in the next room, talking about how I will never succeed. She casts guilt, shame, and hopelessness in my direction. There is nothing wrong with what I do, and I can't understand what these people are so concerned about. The only thing I fear is running out of cocaine. I reload the pipe, inhale, and awake.

❧ 3 ☙

I walk outside and find a dark figure hiding nearby; I am fearful and my body refuses to respond – I am stuck in slow motion while the world around me stays in real time. I awake.

I walk outside and find a dark figure hiding nearby, blocking the path. I tell my friend that it is a demon; he believes and takes me back to the house with urgency.

I am protected.

❧ 4 ☙

"No, don't give them the gate."

❧ 5 ☙

I am standing in a crowded plaza. War has just been declared and I immediately focus on a young blonde girl. I walk up to her and enfold her in my arms. I tell her who I am, what is happening, and ask her to come with me. She makes her choice, and decides to follow me. People are destroying everything they touch; their minds have become tainted. All people disappear – gone somewhere.

I open the stone covering of a shelter beneath me; I know we can stay here and be reasonably protected. Once open, I find the shelter has been filled with trash – filled all the way to the top. I am shocked and disgusted, I am fearful that I will not be able to remove all the trash in time. War is coming; the bombs are in flight. I begin to clear the trash immediately.

Time passes. I am staying in the shelter with a shovel in my hand. I am still clearing away the wreckage and she is with me.

6

I stand in a gathering of people. The bombs have already begun falling.

"I need to go to the Island," I say to them.

"It may no longer exist," one says. "Even if it remains, do you think you could be safe? There is nowhere left to hide."

FLASH. I am in a boat, crossing the water. There is someone with me, but they are scared. "Don't worry", I say, "We'll be there soon." I hit land, and launch into the sky as my boat divides into two swords, which I throw into the ground on either side of me.

7

I go to sleep and awake in a room. I seek the girl I can sense upon waking; we come together and embrace in love. I walk to the sink and try to shave, but I realize the sink has no bottom and the water is pouring out onto the floor. I travel and think,

"I am still asleep." I wake myself and stumble down the hall. I enter my room and realize, "Here we go again." I see through my eyes and awake myself. I hold on to waking with all I have.

8

I am standing outside in the gravel for a smoke break. I lift myself off the ground by focusing my mind. A woman yells at me: "Hey you; I see you; they're coming; I know where you are."

As I walk back into the restaurant, the woman comes rushing inside with another man. They accuse me of stealing from them. I take hold of the man before he has a chance to do anything and say,

David Burton

"Are you sure you want to do this, because when you find out you are wrong…" I finish this sentence with anger burning in my eyes and passion in my heart. "I work in this store and I have no need of your money." I say these words not only to the woman but all who stand inside the restaurant.

"Please do not hold this against this woman because she knows not what she does; she is mistaken."

9

"Do you want my rules?" she asks. "Grieve deeply and honestly – show remorse. Don't offer me your arm; distort [*alter*] time."

10

I find the one I love and she is able to interpret all my art. She asks me to draw from the eyes of the painting rather than from my own and she asks why I only use two series of colors.

Then I hear on the radio she has been murdered and I fucking lose it. I jump into the air and fly, searching for the one who has killed her.

11

"Take up the sword, angel; it is yours by bloodright."

12

I am walking, travelling; yet I am filled with a sense of searching, nearing yet not finding what it is I seek. Symbols begin to emerge: three discs, each bearing wings of flight – each one a different method.

⌘ **13** ⌘

I wake in the middle of the night, and find my body in the depths of sickness. A fever rages inside me, and I shiver with the cold. I rise into the ice air of night, and drink liquid until my thirst vanishes.

I close my eyes, and open them to another world. It is morning. Today is the first day of work, out near the ocean. I look out the window and see the snow falling from the white clouds in the sky above me.

I travel the highway, pulling in where the work office is supposed to be, but instead of finding a building, I find darkness – it descends around me in a cloud. Fires burn in the sudden night, and I hear people laughing, drinking.

I feel compelled to search for the work, so I attempt to walk toward the highway. I see a fire burning in the darkness, surrounded by dark figures. I hear them laughing in the distance, an evil laughter consumed with hatred. I approach the fire to ask for directions but something I see drives me to hold my tongue and I leave quickly.

While crossing the lawn, heading toward the steps I come across a man who has a camera and asks to speak with me. I pause, remove my hood, and listen to his voice. Within seconds two others appear, wanting to give me something. Smoke is brought forth and again I feel compelled to use. I acquiesce to the pressure and get high. Flashing lights appear; these people are scared – terrified – and leave, yet not before placing an object in my pocket.

I race down the steps and emerge into daylight. The highway is before me in full light.

"Why did I do this!?" I scream as all my feelings crash into me. I am distraught at the possibility of losing the contact I have established while dreaming.

"What is wrong?" I hear a woman's voice behind me.

"I… I…" am surprised; a realization begins to form.

David Burton

"What has happened, Risen?"

Suddenly, the world crystallizes in clarity, and I understand that I am *awake*. I explain to her that I have consumed a chemical and I do not know how or why it happened – only that it happened against my will. I must now return and face the consequences; I begin to panic – tears form and sweat is running down my face. I feel high physically. Her eyes are clear. I say,

"How can you know me? I have not met you before. You know me, have we have met before?" I ask.

"Yes."

I begin to explain: "This is very important. The next time you see me I need you to remember: right now I am in bed, far away, asleep." The sweat pours from my body. I know I'm taking a risk in speaking the truth, yet I need to know.

Another girl appears beside me; I am desperately struggling with my mind and body.

"None of this has happened yet," she whispers inside my head as I turn and walk away. The realization has come.

"Where are you going!?" Her voice turns ice cold and begins changing; I turn back to her – her face is tilted forward and one of her eyes blazes with light. It is as if a hole has been punctured in her human form, and light pours form from behind it.

"I must go," my anger is seized by my hand; I embrace the power, and stretch forth my hand. "I must leave now, and if you choose to fight me – you will lose."

She stops, shock registering on her face as she realizes I am not lying. She slides easily beneath my arm and smiles –

"Our side needs one like you."

I leave her with the thought that we need to talk further in the future without the disaster first; yet right now, I must go and warn myself.

I awake in the night and know I have been given a gift. I have seen what will come.

❧ 14 ☙

"*Awake, arise, and ascend.*"

And no marvel; for Satan
himself is transformed into an
angel of light.

2 Corinthians 11:14

David Burton

CHAPTER FOUR

S atan challenged me this afternoon in meditation; he came in the guise of a little girl, slipping through my defenses and whispering in my ear – then once I realized and cast out, he used the old tactic of waking within the dream. In this first waking I immediately fell from meditation to my knees and prayed but I soon realized (due to spacial disorientation) that I was still within the realm, so I wake and once again fall to my knees in prayer.

2

I am standing in the sand on the shore of an ocean, looking out over the water. I stand in darkness and waves come toward me, white caps glowing with light.

FLASH. I fight with one dressed in black, his intentions: to inflict pain. I become frustrated quickly – I reach one hand to the sky and pull a star down into the palm of my hand, throwing it at him as a warning.

FLASH. I stand in corridors of objects. I am searching for something and others search for the same thing, but not for the same reason. I leave the ground; but, the flight is short. The depth of emotion is not present and I do not want to do it for the sake of vanity.

3

In meditation, I find myself in a small room. I am wearing a robe and there is a small song bird in the room with me. I want it to be close to me, so I put my finger out in hope. Surprise overcomes me as it flutters its wings and lands on my fingertip. I am filled with gratitude, surprise, and happiness; I decide to feed it bread and this is where everything falls apart. It sticks its beak into the bread, piercing the skin beneath. I feel pain and try to remove it gently; up it comes and dies from the pressure I exerted. Immediate distress falls upon me. I lay it on the ground; sadness overwhelms me as I try to lift it and its wings break. I try to put it back together and too late I realize that I have resurrected it with the wings not fully healed. I am crying tears as I feel the pain I have inflicted upon the creature. I awake in shock and horror at my actions; actions taken on impulse, without forethought and cascading into trauma with each choice I made.

～❀ 4 ❀～

I am chasing girls, following them from one place to another, seeking them out and trying to fall in love with them. I am seeking a deep and profound emotional connexion with each of them.

～❀ 5 ❀～

I stand on the beach near a crowd of people. I look up to the hillside and see a hole, a cavern. People are climbing out of it. It is a place where people go if they have nowhere else to go, and I can feel its evil emanating outward. Somehow, I end up beside the hole and the crowd is forcing me through the opening. Darkness descends. I am in a room where people are drinking and are naked.

～❀ 6 ❀～

I am on a ship carrying submarines, and other weapons of human warfare, as well as the passengers. We all disembark the vessel. I am with a woman, but she soon disappears. A series of events ends with me hunting a person in the forest and grasslands. I find him, thinking at first that he is dead, but he lives and I take him to a place for refreshment. Someone else is hunting him because he has done something against the culture (that is the impression I am given). I leave the man and seek the hunter, finding him on a hillside beside a stone pathway.

We talk of death. He explains something. His eyes have a tinge to them, a glow; but, it is not one of good – it is something else, otherwise his eyes are dull and distant. I tell him something of death and leave him standing there.

I come across another man in the woods standing near a local shrine. There is a stone covered in moss. Underneath the moss is a circular inscription of the word '*kill*' repeating, with strange symbols between the words. When I see this I realize that the people are consumed and I must leave this place quickly and quietly.

It is too late; already they pursue us. They chase us in human form, but I sense the evil within them. We go to a house where I find a man who is willing to hide us. He is speaking with us when one of those we seek to escape walks out of the woods. I react quickly, although others are fooled by his guise.

"He has led them to us," I yell. Some believe; others do not. I run. The woods come crashing down and a small force emerges to slaughter the waiting people. It is horror. I wake, kneel and pray.

❧ 7 ☙

I am trying out different jobs at which I am neither afraid to steal, quit or speak my mind. I steal from the rich and speak out against injustice – demonstrating to others that they need not become slaves to their employer.

FLASH. I am standing in a cavern with shallow water and prostitution; evil dwells here.

FLASH. I am in another city. I am abducted by a group of people and threatened. My mind totally accepts Satan's lie – I forget who I am. I feel sick; this dream is twisted. Help abandons me and I'm left alone with a group of people. We walk until they are eventually arrested. I return to a place where I was before and explain why I disappeared. I feel guilty because it was beyond my control, yet I could have chosen differently.

FLASH. I am saved and the group scatters, but I hunt them down and retrieve the ring I lost. I give them grace because they were dealing with an evil beyond their understanding. Satan played on my fears and took advantage of my inability to see through his lies. The ring was blue stone, set in silver, in the shape of an eye.

8

I leave my recovery to go score some crack cocaine. When I return to the house, I realize I don't have a pipe, so I eat it. As soon as the taste hits my mouth I realize what is happening and run to the bathroom, spitting it out of my mouth and into my hands as I run. I am terrified that even this small taste will show up on a drug test. I am puking into the sink as the house leader walks by the open doorway, showing a new resident the house.

9

I run across the room and drive my fist into a man's chest, saying: "What have I done that has hardened your heart so!?"

10

I am in the woods, on a farm with a small ring of cabins. Demons have surrounded the area, and are trying to pierce our defenses. People are scared, but my attention is on the beautiful girl at my side. I am focused on taking her clothes off, and less worried about the evil presence trying to kill us all.

I awake, forget the dream, and carry on with my day. The dream returns to me while I am outside smoking in the rain. Anger surges within me, and I cry out:

"You come for me!?" I am angry that demons would come against me. I feel challenged, my authority questioned and the outermost tinge of rage – I want to scream.

11

I dream of a girl that I have fallen in love with years ago. I am unsure whether to touch her, because it has been a long while since our last contact. I am scared she will reject me or withhold her touch because of her anger. She walks toward me and we kiss. I love her so much; she has not aged – she is beautiful; I want to cry. I want her hand in mine; I want to run my fingers through her hair, and pull her body against mine. I have not seen her in a long time and I am fighting to hold on to the time we have. We enter a tent and I move close to her, for warmth, closeness, protection, comfort. I zip shut the tent door as darkness falls. Soon, I can begin to feel her leaving. It feels like my soul is slipping away, going to a different place, and leaving me here. I wake shortly afterward.

I love her so much. The way her scent travels on the wind, the silk softness of her hair falling around her face. When our hands are linked I feel complete in many ways; there is no malice in her heart, or mind – only a tinge of fear that the world will not accept us.

❦ 12 ❦

I go back to the other world, and she appears immediately. This time we come together without hesitation. She is so beautiful, inside and outside.

❦ 13 ❦

I get off the ground, testing my bounce, pre-flight, and balance.

❦ 14 ❦

I am writing a book with a girl in another world. She is really upset that I have stopped writing, and urges me to continue.

Thrilling in its possible devastation; addiction is knowing the outcome and pursuing the cause in spite of knowledge. Crack is a stone with many facets.

❦ 15 ❦

I am with a girl and we are trying to become one, but an evil force keeps interfering – he comes as a man. Eventually, I become so angry I run to the cliff side, and launch myself into the sky. I land on a log jam that has completely blocked a river. The logs roll and spin as I walk across. I grab hold of one and pull – the key to the entire jam. I realize quickly what I've done and run to the shore.

FLASH. I am making breakfast in the kitchen with someone else; she gives me a strange glance which catches my attention. I look down and see my daughter with her arms raised, crying – I pick her up with love in my heart and say,

"If you want to be in my arms, why didn't you say anything?" She wouldn't even have to say it out loud.

FLASH. I am in a school hallway, waiting for the girl. She is trying to get permission for us to study together.

16

I watch a fight between a master fighter and a young man; the man falls to the ground wounded severely. I immediately respond, thinking the man is dead. I am in crouch position, my eyes burning, waiting to see if the man will rise. To my surprise, he rises. I relax and walk with the master fighter back to his house. I project my thoughts to him and we talk about mysteries: I explain to him that fighting style [*learning, living*] is like "seeing a painting" and then painting another. I awake singing, "Holy, Holy, Holy."

17

I dream I have a long beard and I am trying to save a girl from the emotional pain she is experiencing. I have an overwhelming urge to take her in my arms and hold her close to my heart. I awake before I have the chance.

18

I am in the kitchen and put my hand in my pocket. I am taught how to create coin by swirling my hand around, searching for what is already there. I take it and throw it on the counter. It is not the money that has any importance, but the gift of finding (creating) it; still the man with me does not believe.

I ask for his cigarette package, give him the last smoke, close and shake the package – I open it full of cigarettes.

I learn to give faith to others, to show them God loves, cares for, and is here with them, among them, from them.

Faith is *believing* there is something already in your pocket. It's *knowing* that God has given a gift and he will not take it away. A circle gathers around me as I continue to show these works.

I take an empty bag of candy and shake it, believing it will be filled, and it is – I throw it to someone in the crowd. It is then that I see one of the people with chains around their neck, standing on a black symbol. He refuses to believe no matter what sign is given. I ask him to remove the chains, but he will not – he is ashamed. He leaves the group.

I am given the ability to sign someone off to sleep; they take a single step and fall to the ground.

At the end, I am walking with two women. I ask one for tea, as she is beautiful – filled with love and innocence. We enter a room behind a glass door. When the door closes I fall to my knees in agony and exhaustion, my head pounds with pain.

"It is finally quiet." The minds of the people and the crowd have overwhelmed me because I sense, I *hear* – all. I awake and pray.

᠅ 19 ᠅

I am in a battle, a war, in which I meet a beautiful woman who asks me to wipe certain sections of her mind. During the process she loses movement of her body. A man is trying to kill her. I struggle with him violently and kill him, saving her. I embrace my rage. I take her in my arms and I feel her body against mine. I would have leveled a city for her; I would have destroyed a world to protect our love. Her voice is pure, innocent – she trusts me.

᠅ 20 ᠅

Last night I fought a battle; it was strange – I don't want to write about it. This morning I awake and my eyes are glowing green then blue. This is the sign I've been waiting for.

✎ 21 ✎

I am on a bus, travelling across the countryside. I am standing in a puddle of water inside the vehicle, and I wear a cross around my neck. My feet are bare; water laps against my skin.

All the boys spark a joint and circle around me, passing it from person to person. It comes to me and I wave it off. It passes around the circle and the boy next to me tries to hand it to me again. I decline once more. As it travels around the circle for the final time I sense the fury rising within me. I can smell it burning. This time he places it right close to my face and I freak.

"If you put that joint in my face one more time, I will fucking kill you." I say it with force and solidity; I have not a single doubt in any part of me. I've changed. I awake, fall to my knees and pray.

✎ 22 ✎

"I am surprised and shocked at this project you undertake."

✎ 23 ✎

A demon tortures me, lashing my body. I fight with love. I try to *love* the demon away. It does not work, so fuck this idea – I won't try it again.

✎ 24 ✎

I am unable to sleep; my dreams are filled with demons, everywhere. I prayed and read the written word before sleep – I have been asleep for one hour and it has been days within the dream. The closer I come to God, the more Satan throws at me.

✎ 25 ✎

I awake in another world. I hold my infant child in my arms. I am with a girl, but our relationship is falling apart. Our child learns how to talk incredibly fast and walks in days. At one point, we try to catch

David Burton

a ride home on the bus. Someone decides to take us out into the middle of nowhere.

"Take us home; we have a child who was born yesterday." I scream at him, furious. I have rage burning within me and I want to kill him. We eventually return home. I awake. Our child in my arms vanishes with the coming dawn and I am alone. I feel empty.

26

I stand on the edge of a building, thousands of feet in the air, trying to get the elevator to go down. I nearly fall and I am blown off the edge. I grasp the building with my fingertips. I phase and find myself in a hallway with many pictures scattered on the ground.

FLASH. I am with a girl and we come together in strength. We marry and travel the earth. We have a child together and I fight for them. And, out of nowhere, a satellite in space that shines on a planet that burns red, glowing black. The imaging system is alive and speaks to me.

27

I am in a foreign country; I leave the city to gather warriors, and return with them beneath the bridge.

FLASH. I am standing on the street and a fight breaks out; I step in and put an end to it. I am filled with strength that is not my own.

"Stop fighting amongst yourselves," I scream and awake. I fall to my knees and pray.

28

I am attacked by demonic forces in the first three minutes of the night. The demons are standing around a brimstone fire, calling me toward them. No fucking way. I awake saying,

"In the name of our Lord and Saviour Jesus Christ, I cast thee out."

Today, as every day, I awake just before dawn. I rise and walk outside into the coming daylight.

❧ 29 ☙

I am in the shower with a girl. "It's okay," she says, "you can leave now." I step out and awake instantly.

❧ 30 ☙

I see her in the night and I am watching her undress when she notices me. She invites me over and I get naked. We have sex; it is amazing. She is vivid, clear and in contact.

❧ 31 ☙

I am dreaming of my kitten, Storm. He gets trapped in a net and I rush to free him. I hold him in my arms and heal him. He has a patch of blood on his fur. I feel connected to him in a way I am unable to describe, but is crystal clear. I play with him and feel love. I am his protector and warrior – when he needs me, I am there.

❧ 32 ☙

I am in part of the city in which I do not belong. I give cigarettes away to people who need them. Many people come to approach me and give me gifts; one man says,

"You are a White King." I feel called to another place, so I go.

When I arrive I battle a person from a distance. He throws boomerang like objects at me. The first and second pass by each side of me; he prepares two more. I turn my back on him, and use *faith*. I *believe* these weapons will not touch me. I *hear* them pass by around each side of me, hit each other and fall to the ground. The fifth time he throws I turn, catch it and send it back at him – embedding it in his heart: the battle is over.
I look around me and I see the earth, water and plant life as though I were miles above the surface of the earth. I turn to one side and see a creature ascending a stairway. I do not feel threatened but a

part of me experiences the terror of first contact. The creature has tattoos on its arms, and is wearing a robe. Its hair is white, sweeping up and back off its head. Weird. It glides, it does not walk. On either side of me are lakes or seas, miles below. I see a long and curved rod like a track. Planes circle around it and I understand that they are moved by magnetics. The flight exercise ends and they are pulled into docking position on the central rod.

33

A group of us walk along a mountain range. I look at the water below, the shore, the trees and other movement. As darkness falls, I tell them to,

"Stay away from the edge for it can be deceiving. You can walk right off without knowing it."

FLASH. I am at a party where I meet a beautiful girl. We talk, we touch – she takes me to her room. She shows me her journal and I see a picture of my human form inside it, with her. I am confused. She takes me downstairs and someone comes after us. I stop in front of her, shielding, and make it very clear to the man that he is never to return, lest I pierce him. I do this by placing my finger against his neck and pushing it to the wall.

There are other devices in this room. The girl and I have the same thought: "Depth can happen with trust." We can explore each other further sexually and otherwise only with faith and trust. I give her my life, and she gives me hers.

34

I find her in a field and we travel to an enclosed space; I want her close to me. We are there for some time, yet we are interrupted as usual.

FLASH. We come together again in the darkness – the world is ending and creatures have taken over. As we run I tell her to remove her clothes and I tear mine off. We run to a corner of darkness, naked, and roll in the disgusting mess of earth, letting our lust carry us with no inhibition. When the creatures come they allow us to live, whether because we did as they or because they could not sense the difference. I don't know. We run out of the darkness and into the light. There we find an abandoned world, where only the machines that govern themselves remain. We climb into a car and drive away.

FLASH. I travel far to come to her house – the world is not yet destroyed, but is changing. I enter her house and wrap my arms around her; she does not mention that she has a man trying to own her. He appears with his followers and threatens violence. I forget who I am and fear him. His illusion is cast over me and I leave her there because of my fear.

We separate and I travel the earth. I see creatures I have not seen before and avoid them. Eventually time phases and I am standing in her office years later as she frees herself from the man. It comes to a climax in a single scene. He comes to her place of work and tries to impose his will. I can no longer allow it for I am stronger and I have a champion who fights with me.

He shows me the way, running toward the demon. He calls on the power and pulses a ball of white fire from his hand. The pulse pushes the demon back through the glass, shattering the window. As the demon falls to the ground below, my champion leaps into the sky, descending and landing upon the broken body below. I follow and the man's reign of terror is ended.

❦ 35 ❧

We are upon the ocean; our boats are anchored. The weapon fires continuously, launching our projectiles against an island. They come crashing into the ground. The weapon fires so fast that it bursts into flames. It ends and occurs again as this process continues. The land collapses into the sea.

FLASH. I am beneath the sea with the girl; she is the focus of my love and I tell her so. We kiss and our arms are wrapped around each other. She begins to worry about time, and I tell her not to fear because I can breathe and time does not matter. We have been given time.

David Burton

36

I fight with an invisible [*unseen*] man, and find two dragons trying to pass through an underwater portal.

FLASH. I battle wolves that change into creatures.

38

I am walking around a distant town and come across a girl. I enter an abandoned house, finding only one person standing within – an evil presence that refuses to leave. I pull a sword from nothing and put it through his heart.

FLASH. I am at a house on the beach and there is a party happening. I find a girl, take her in my arms and walk over to the couch. I place her down and take off her black shorts; we will fuck – we are in the throes of passion. I feel lust, and I love it.

39

Two keys around my neck: one to open the outer door and another to open the inner door.

40

I am walking toward the ocean and I hear people singing; there is a choir standing on the sand. I approach and listen. I feel uplifted. The gathered crowd honours several people but they ridicule me, saying: "Look at him, he is all alone: he has no one." I turn and leave. I put my hood up and pull my jacket around me.

❧ 41 ❧

A few dreams came and they were strong. I flew, I fought evil, I awoke, I slept, I travelled far away. In one place I meet a girl who desires me. I take her into a private room and begin removing her clothes. She is laying in front of me, wearing only her panties, when she says,

"Don't do this." I don't understand, everything about her screams sex and willingness, but then at the last second, with her pants off, she says these words and I awake.

FLASH. I stand on the ocean shore with my father, looking out over the waves. I ask him if he sails out around the Island or between it and the shore. He says, "Between," and I am relieved because the Island acts as a breaker and offers some protection from the storm.

❧ 42 ❧

I am at the restaurant for a lunch meeting with the staff, and I am clean; everything is sharp and clear. I feel amazing. I walk to the back to relax for awhile, and see symbols hanging on chains. One in particular stands out, a *taijitu* covered in flames and lightning bolts. I don't know how to explain this. I feel crystal clear, present, conscious, aware and alive.

AWAKE.

For the flesh lusteth against
the Spirit, and the Spirit
against the flesh: and these are
contrary the one to the other:
so that ye cannot do the things
ye would.

Galatians 5:17

David Burton

CHAPTER FIVE

I am fighting with someone about my son and the amount of weed he is smoking. I take the weed and say, "I'll *know* when he is smoking too much," implying that I have had years of experience. "However, I'm keeping the weed." I send my son out of the room so that I can engage the conversation. I sit down and begin rolling. We are going to sit, smoke and talk.

FLASH. We are out for lunch somewhere with someone; people are drinking a grape wine, and I finally have a glass. I can't describe the taste but it is amazing – it explodes, sending sensations flowing through my mind. I purchase a bottle and awake. When I fall asleep again I dream of a vine upon which is a fruit that once picked, ever increases.

2

I am trying to fix some light bulbs.

FLASH. I am walking past a bus stop and a young girl follows me, wanting to be away from the people that are bothering her. There is a long wall stretching across the land with a single gate. As we approach the opening the girl leans against the wall and crouches down. Her face is fallen with sadness.

"We must pay," she says.

"It is free," I reply. "Come, follow me." I open the gate and we enter. She puts her arm around me and I put my arm around her. We become one together and walk across the grass. She looks into my eyes, gently, sexy – and we kiss. At this point the urge to have sex takes over, but my alarm awakens me as we are about to consecrate.

3

I meet a girl, standing beside the ocean. She is wearing a white shirt and flower panties. We are destined to be together. Eventually, we enter the water, and touch each other. We begin to kiss, and she wants to have sex as much as I. Our arms are wrapped around each other, but I feel the waking coming on; I hold off waking until we are united, and I awake.

4

Two beautiful women are fighting over who is the most beautiful – one is evil, one is good. The evil one tries to incite the good one, which makes her beauty void and ugly. My eyes lock with the good one and I try to convey the message that I support and love her, the only problem is that she has expressed interest in someone near me, a dark figure from the opposing side. I tell her that in the future everything will be alright, but she has to choose me first because I have already chosen her.

5

A girl is trying to contact me; we are connected in ways I don't yet understand.

FLASH. My entire face is covered in white cloth except for my eyes, and blood stains the cloth.

6

I awake knowing nothing: where I am, who I, what day it is – NOTHING. I speak aloud.

7

I have many dreams moving toward a singular event which I can't remember. There is a battle where I quote words from a text. I fight for the girl's freedom. The whole thing is blurry and unclear.

8

I am in a city where everything is very strange. The walls and sky are video screens which play images. As I am walking through this city, I look up, and see a fighter jet transform into a shuttle craft.

David Burton

"It is a phantom jet." Demons appear, and the war continues, as I fight them on the ground. In frustration I launch myself into the air, spreading my wings.

FLASH. A shape shifter trying to break in.

FLASH. I am making supper with evil people in a wooden finished house. They look good on the outside, but their kitchen sink is filled with dirty water and disgusting dishes. Their rooms are a gross mess. The two women are talking about going to the Island and they are asking me to accompany them.

I awake and begin singing to dispel the darkness and thank the Lord for my wings.

9

I meet someone named, "Aeon." She is gifted with the ability of being present without being seen. I have known her for a very long time, but I can't remember ever having met her. I see her one day in the hallways of a school; she is young, while I have aged. She rarely comes close to me, but I find a way to be near her and I call her by her true name. I see the surprise and shock register on her face as I finish speaking.

"Ten years from now you will fall in love," I say to her. She quickly guesses who it is she will fall in love with, and she suddenly understands why I know her name.

Her shock changes to joy and we engage in a game that only we can play. We alter time and move through the hallways of the school at unknown speeds. Time has been suspended in the world, but for us it is just another day.

10

I am in a recycling plant where people bring their old computer systems for disposal. I take apart the old systems, removing the parts I need in order to build a new system. When I have completed the task, I take the new system with me.

A man approaches me and begins to lecture me on my work; he says it is wrong to take what does not belong to me and that it goes against my belief as a Christian.

"You can't steal that which is given away freely," I reply. "Let me explain this to you. I will only do it once. You, as a people, have lost scripture. When people read scripture they see *words on a page*. I read the verse and just *know*. This called the *living word*."

I turn to walk away from the man and find that the system I built has now become a sword, capable of building or destroying the world.

∽❦ 11 ❧∾

I am with a girl who touches her forehead to mine in order to communicate. The contact allows her to speak inside my mind. With a glance, she shapeshifts into a cat and then bows to me. I am shocked and unsure of how to proceed.

FLASH. I am standing on the top floor of a building in a city far away. Water begins pouring into the streets and the city floods, all the way up several floors.

∽❦ 12 ❧∾

I run from place to place planting roses in the garden and talking to people. I finally come to her house, it is different, I can sense her within. I open the door and find her standing inside. Our eyes meet, hers glow blue and intense. Our eyes come together several times. I show her my soul, desire, longing and love, projecting them with my mind. Coming together, we touch.

Suddenly people burst into our world, invading our privacy. I stand firm and command them to leave. Creatures follow after these people, coming for us all, and many are forced to flee. I stand and fight the onslaught of creatures; I fight to protect her. I fight because I love her, and after years of searching I have finally found her.

❧ 13 ☙

I achieve *iceberg quality oneness with the universe* – in other words: I feel amazing, as though some gift of knowledge has been bestowed upon me. I do not remember the specific events of the dream; the overall feeling, however, is beautiful and inspiring.

❧ 14 ☙

I am shopping in a grocery store. I buy some and steal some; it all goes in the same bag. After paying for the items I walk the streets, trying to give it away – it all goes to someone who needs it. I hear a voice echoing inside my mind, saying,

"I have given more than is required, and *abundantly*, when I only needed to give a little."

FLASH. I unfold a photograph from my pocket. It is a negative. It is a picture of a planet, a star chart. There are numbers scrawled in the space around the stars.

❧ 14 ☙

I am in a church, and I steal money from the offering basket. The congregation joins together in an attempt to kill me. I defend myself from their attack, hurting many of them in the process.

I have a book that they try to take because it opens a gateway to another world.

❧ 15 ☙

I had a significant dream but I awake with no memory it; no thread, even, to weave. It is as though an eraser was taken to it. I cry. There was a locked door.

❧ **16** ❧

I have *awakened*. She is here, she is clear, she is beautiful, and she is present – she was unseen, yet now is seen.

❧ **17** ❧

I dream of a singer, a beautiful young girl who is amazing and talented. She tells me it is all a cover, a way to hide what she really is. She is a star fighter pilot, an ace of the skies, flight leader. We are under attack and I am wiring her stereo for sound. She loves to listen to music while she flies. We are connected somehow and I love her.

❧ **18** ❧

I am in a three section auditorium. I am there to hear my friend speak to an all female class. There is also a tower with a spiral staircase and someone is knocking at the door, trying to draw me out.

❧ **19** ❧

I wake up talking about *'causation;'* something to do with cause and effect. The dream itself has slipped away temporarily.

❧ **20** ❧

I am in prison, not understanding why I am here. I leave the prison, escaping into the night. They know I have escaped and send people to find and kill me. Soon they are upon me and the fight ensues. I feel the knife cut two wounds in my arm. At this point, I am left alone with the leader and I hurt him badly enough to paralyze him.

I weep, not for my wounds, but for the one I inflict upon him.

21

I am space jumping, and it is intense. I fall from a platform in space, racing toward the earth. I land upon the earth and find a war raging all around me. I am enlisted in an army and sent on an assignment. A military craft appears, hovering in the sky above the ground. The craft appears empty, so our team boards it to obtain intelligence. Out of nowhere, the enemy appears and pushes one of our soldiers out the side door.

There is no time to consider options, he is falling to earth below and will surely be destroyed upon impact. I leap from the craft into the sky, falling quickly. The moment I lay hands on the soldier falling through the air below me I teleport us both to safety.

FLASH. I meet someone with a translator; somewhere among all this, I search for something I can't seem to grasp, and she is nearby.

22

I travel and come across a section of land where tents have been raised in the late autumn grass. In the center of the camp there is a tent that controls all the others. All the poles have rope running to a central sling, in which a rock is suspended midair. I ask the people what the significance of this creation is, and I am told that it is a shelter for people in the way.

FLASH. I am standing on the balcony of the girl's place, overlooking the parking lot when I see a car pull up. There are three people in the vehicle, a man in the center and two girls on either side. The women are *fake* and submit to evil, their gestures give them away. It is as though I am watching a play from a distance.

I turn, fuck the girl and awake.

23

I travel to many cities and am rejected of man. Eventually, I find a girl in the forest who has written a book. I fall in love with her. I see the ocean somewhere beyond the edge of the forest.

✤ **24** ✤

I am in an Egyptian temple underground. I have found the entrance that has lain buried for countless years. The doorway has been opened and now others are trying to gain access. I know what lay beyond and am not quick to enter. The rest is faded.

✤ **25** ✤

I found flight last night and it was beautiful. I fought although I lost memory of it. There was frustration in other segments and it ended with me holding the jaws of a creature closed in my hands.

✤ **26** ✤

All night long I live in a world far from this one; before dawn I return and awake. Time is meaningless – I will always be as such.

✤ **27** ✤

I am standing at the podium. I see a girl from my past, she is with her other significant. I have slept with this girl in the past, interfering with their relationship. When I finish speaking, she approaches me and we start talking. She moves in close and gives me a quick kiss, just as her friend turns around.

He comes over and starts yelling at me, but I stand my ground. I am innocent of any further offence. I simply try to ignore the man, but my lack of response enrages him further.

He swings at me with his fist, but I weave and send him sprawling with the power inside of me. He falls to the floor, and I walk quickly to where he lay. I stand over him, my hand on his chest, restraining him. I see the fear in his eyes.

"Stop, hold on, let me think." I pick him up off the ground and place him on his feet. A look of confusion crosses his face. I pull him close, hug him, and start crying.

David Burton

"I am sorry. I am truly sorry," I say. I cry and cry; I awake and continue crying. I am sorry for my actions and harm I caused him by sleeping with his girlfriend.

My heart is broken by what I've done.

28

The world is ending, being invaded and bombed. People are being taken and killed. I protect my niece from the war and the evil of this world. Their ships descend from the sky, and I know when.

FLASH. I go to a girl's house. We fall in love. Her child is missing and we go in search of her.

FLASH. I am in an underground stone building which is incomplete; I am searching, walking through passages and pathways. All of these dreams are disturbing. Someone appears in the dream and we begin a conversation.

While I am speaking, I shift between awake and asleep. I can't tell the difference between my two states of awareness. I speak to someone, and they speak to me.

FLASH. A ship descends from the sky; the people [*creatures*] on board are throwing fireballs at the earth.

FLASH. The end of the world comes in a snowfall. I watch as the animals fall to the ground and die.

For if a man thinks himself to
be something, when he is
nothing, he deceiveth himself.

Galatians 6:3

David Burton

CHAPTER SIX

I am walking in the snow behind a few beautiful young women when one of them comes along side of me and starts talking. She loves me and as we are walking, our hands entwine. We pass some people standing by the side of the road.

"Do you want to see them, or come with me?" I ask. She is surprised by my directness. She answers; we continue. She tells me about the guitar player.

FLASH. I am in a room when I notice something is missing or incomplete; as soon as I formulate this thought, the room changes and the missing object appears.

~ **2** ~

I am standing in an old building with many floors. The floors are filled with rooms, finished in the Victorian style. I am in the presence of a demon; I can sense it nearby. I find its place of hiding and bind into between the pages of a book. The book bursts into flames.

I run to the window and throw open the glass pane. I notice a car pulling up in front of the building, and know this is my chance to leave. I run out of the room, into the hall, and down the stairs. As I approach the door on the ground floor level, I notice an old man standing near the entrance. He is weathered, and looks to have been standing there for years. His eyes lock with mine.

"The door can't open," he says.

"The spell has been broken," I reply as I push the glass door open, and walk outside. I am leaving and nothing can stop me.

~ **3** ~

I am standing on a platform made of iron on the sea. It has four quadrants and circle marked center. There is a vehicle on the platform. I am moving objects, searching for something I do not find. I walk off the platform onto steady ground.

FLASH. I am walking and talking with a girl. I am throwing pieces of fruit into the holes of the earth, sowing. I go for coffee with a girl who keeps telling me to leave because of the people who are coming for coffee, or are at coffee with us already.

~ **4** ~

We are working on a building with angled sides and windows hidden beneath the layers. An explosion of wind, heat, fire, smoke and ash comes blowing across the face of the earth. I fall to the concrete and shield myself against the pain. I hold my breath and do not breathe because the air is poison.

FLASH. I find myself in a large cavern; it has light and vast space. A girl is with me, standing silent at my side. There is a stairway carved into the rock, descending into the earth. A door stands open at the top of the staircase, and another at the bottom. Hidden rooms line the stairs. In one of these rooms there is a book which is the key to the guitar, life, and everything else.

"This is the *living word*," I say to her. "Do you understand? It can talk to you if it decides to, or ignore you like any other person." I am to keep and protect this book, and its power.

~ **5** ~

I am near the ocean and I step over a small rock wall to get closer to the beach. As I approach, a white horse comes running toward me. He neighs and screams at the wind; he nudges me with his head and then pushes. I start running as he runs behind me and lifts me from the ground. I am now flying faster than I can imagine through the field.

FLASH. There is a girl who is with me and is having a hard time believing in me because her father [*the world*] keeps projecting lies to her, saying that I am somehow guilty until proven innocent.

David Burton

❦ 6 ❧

I see a stone bridge standing in the darkness of night, stretching over a small river. There are two young lions with glowing eyes guarding the bridge. So, I try to cross beneath the bridge, through the water and the stones. The lions follow and come to me. I ask them what they want of me and if they are going to allow me to cross.

FLASH. I am walking a pathway near the railway in late autumn and snow begins to fall. I see a girl standing near the trees. I reach down into the snow and gather it into my hands. I throw a snowball at her and we exchange a few small words.

FLASH. I cross the bridge: there are doors on both sides. I feel naked as I walk across the stone structure. On the other side I see the girl again, but this time she is just turning past the age of puberty. Again we speak.

FLASH. The rain is falling as I stand in a dark world. I see a tall chain link fence stretching into the night. A girl is sitting on the bench, near the cold steel fence. I walk toward her because I have come for her, I love her. Her skin is changing and she has aged dramatically. I take her in my arms, and reassure her. Her clothes are soaked and she is shivering. I take her to my house and give her dry clothes.

FLASH. Someone comes in and tries to make me feel guilty for helping her but I ignore it. Something happens, someone comes, and we are forced to flee once again. We enter an aircraft, leaving the earth behind. I see the army below that will follow us. I call on the power, placing lightning into the machine and it changes. I tell her to remain while I go to the ground to finish things.

❦ 7 ❧

I am fighting with my father.

FLASH. A girl rises up off the ground near me. I am angry and excited to prove myself to her. I extend my hands and feel lift; yet, not enough. She rises and touches down gracefully. I reach up above my head and interlace my fingers. I soar upward toward the power lines. I touch a line and sparks fly, yet it is a soothing current running through my body. I touch another line and descend to the ground. The landing is not graceful; however, the excitement within me is awesome.

"And that is just a beginning of what I can do with the power." I tell my father, who has come to help me out of the ditch I fell into while landing.

8

Demons come and try to take my guitar away. Now I am pissed off beyond anything I've ever known. I'll never let them silence or illusion me again.

9

I am on my spaceship with a girl; we are taking it back from the enemy. I find the flight controls and we fly.

10

I find an old book with pictures of water creatures, and of a meadow, near the water with sun rays shining down on it. The book is about trying to explain about *communication* with something beyond what is understood by man.
It is a theory. A woman is looking at it. I get the feeling she is pleased, asking me to revisit the theory and perhaps change it to add the knowledge I have now.

FLASH. I am in an underground cavern, which is for escape. It has a vehicle that speeds away toward an unknown destination.

11

I am on the ferry. The crossing is slow, and the vessel is late arriving. The engine has broken down, and they won't let anyone else board.

When they finish repairs, the ship fires up and races across the ocean, leaving huge waves breaking against the shore.

FLASH. I am in a building in an apartment; she arrives and it is at the turning point in her life – willing to let me become a part of it. We love, share, speak, communicate with our minds and body.

FLASH. We are at the ocean's edge and it is frozen; however, the ice is breaking, fluctuating – rising and falling. People fear the water, they fear crossing it, walking on it. I laugh with joy in my heart and jump out onto the ice.

12

There is a gateway upon which is the head of a lion, and this gateway is alive. I find it in the ground of a barren land with a single structure standing beside it. The lion speaks to me, and I stand before it screaming,

"What do you want from me!?" Three times I scream this question, beating my fists upon the image until the rock cracks and falls into the earth.

Once the gate is open, sections of the building immediately fall inward, dissolving, and I realize that the gateway is not singular. It is more a seal than anything, and once broken, the vail is torn. Dark angels are about to come forth, escaping from their prison below, unless I stand against them.

I have now become the guardian of the gateway.

13

I am in a field of wheat. Several trees stand near the edge of the field. In the sky above me is a propeller driven craft of some kind, being followed by a helicopter. As disturbing as it is I don't freak out until I see the carriers – triangular shaped objects, yet rectangular from the bottom. I see several and this is when I start running out into the field, screaming,

"They built them." I know this is a sign of what is to come so I look above the clouds and see the truth: thousands of ships, each with an equilateral triangular opening on the bottom. I watch in awe as they turn, drop and engage their engines.

FLASH. I am on the bridge of the flag ship of the fleet. I am standing behind a woman who is about to cause serious havoc on our planet until she senses it – there is someone on this planet she knows. She parts her long hair, and at the base of her neck there is a tattoo.

৺ **14** ৶

I am in a boat on the sea and I put my hands out into the water. I press down and believe in my mind, heart that the water will solidify in that place for me. The first attempt is shaky; however, the next one works, like the air – water is the same. I reach out behind me and lean on the water. It supports me. I then try to walk on it; yet I am not ready.

৺ **15** ৶

I find a girl as I walk the pathway of worlds. She has been bound in darkness, but I have come to free her from the life she has been living. She helps and encourages me. I teach her as she teaches me. There comes a time when her past seeks her out and attempts to kill us both. The living dead and their vain attempts to hook mankind in their vanity.

As the demon tries to imprison us in water she informs him that he does not know what he is dealing with. Our love breaks the spell of the prison. We escape only to be attacked by another source: the humans and their technology. We are captured and taken to a military facility.

While in their new facility, a man appears and teaches me how to move through objects, taking their power and converting them: he is white and shining.

❦ 16 ❧

I am walking through the city, from here to there. I walk in some situations that scare me; however, I trust and contain. Eventually I come to a library and a wall of vials. I choose one that has my name on it and a picture of an angel. I take the vial and start to walk away when I see a girl approach the wall and take a vial. I follow her out of the city and through an airport.

❦ 17 ❧

I am standing on the ice near the ocean. The sun shines bright, reflecting off the water and ice.

FLASH. I am standing in the center of a forest inside a clearing. There is a black sky above me filled with starlight. I am playing guitar and singing.

{awake} : I place the key inside the lock. I take up the guitar; I sing and play. As I do so, the dream unlocks inside my mind.

❦ 18 ❧

We protected someone long ago and took something he was trying to steal. He never forgot, or forgave us. He came back, still searching. He came after my friends: one is in the sea, tied in a net. I went to the council, to speak before the appointed. I turned away from the gift and plead my case with emotion. The one in the judgment seat walked out half way through.

"Light your light," I said. Then I took the flame from the air and torched the bridge he was walking on. I began the hunt. I told those I knew about what was happening, what was coming. I travelled from world to world, spreading the message.

In one such realm, I search and find a replica of the white stone carving – it shows the torture of the innocent on one side with evil screaming for them to fail, and the guilty on the other side with evil screaming for them to succeed.

I run from the replica, out of the room and find two older ladies outside the door. I say,

"These are God's children, and right now I need you to focus your minds on Him."

Then I turn, take several steps and teleport [**FLASH**]; I bounce through one world, teleport again and find myself in the evil world. I am here to rescue the man and woman. I run around the dirt oval until I find them.

When I find them the evil ones come. They try to kill me, cut me with serrated knives. One tries to hide a blade in his sleeve and pretends he is here to help. I kill them all. A gateway opens to my right and I know friends have finally come. Beyond the gate is a furious storm driven ocean, waves crashing, and a platform.

20

We are in the auditorium and there is a concert taking place. I don't understand the music so I go to the lost and found where I find a game in Chinese, or Japanese. I play until several girls are beside me. And then the world begins to end. There is flooding and the mountains are breaking. We tie ourselves together with rope and start walking.

FLASH. I am standing inside a room with a beautiful woman. Her eyes are like two suns blazing light. As we look at each other, three people enter the house.

"We are here for the meeting," one of them says.

"I don't know how long I can stay," I say. "I am awake within two worlds, at the same time. The philosophy we study is not just a theory. It is a reality. Once we awaken, we are never the same again."

"Perhaps you could speak first," one of them suggests.

"Not him," says one of the others.

David Burton

❧ 21 ❧

I ride the elevator from floor to floor, from world to world and at each stop I find a person. I acquire several people and I realize I must return them to their respective worlds in the reverse sequential order as I acquired them in; otherwise, I condemn them to eternal wandering.

FLASH. As I am returning one girl, I decide to walk with her and solve the problem. I love her and walk with her into the text: her father, the evil one who attempts to control her, sees us and tries to place her into the role she has always played. He threatens violence. It does not matter because now she has met me, and I fight for and protect those I love. I fight and kill the man in order to set her free. **FLASH**. I return to the elevator and finish doing what I have started.

{awake} : I remember running my hands over her body. I can feel her skin beneath my fingertips, I can sense her in my mind and feel her body pressed against mine. Intense and clear.

FLASH. I return to a world and watch a girl solve a mystery. She knows her prey so well that she retraces the steps of the one she pursues. She comes to a flight of stairs and a wall. She takes a pen of some sort and black light. She shines it on the wall, revealing a map and plan of her opponent.

❧ 22 ❧

I marry a young woman, and travel up north to settle a dispute from the past. I encounter my old master, the teacher of my youth. Someone enters the room and threatens him. He is a person from the past. I get his attention and he attacks with a blade. He is strong but I am more so. I cause him to place an ice pick in his head, shattering his skull – he repeatedly stabs himself. The old war is over and I return to my wife.

❧ 23 ❧

I am on a ship. They send someone to communicate with me, but I find out they have really been sent to capture or kill me. The power to the bottom half of the ship has been cut or interrupted, so I explain to the girl that we will have to drop in.

FLASH. I enter a room to confront someone about the power of a certain book and where it has gone. He tries denial but I go to where it was hidden and find it missing.

FLASH. I go and preach the glory and brightness of God to those living in darkness. As I am leaving, an entity reveals its presence. I call on God, at first trying to wake myself. I can barely speak, yet think I am audible. I hear a person in my room respond, but I do not wake. I call on God again; soon, I wake and call on Jesus – then I realize I need to use his name right at the beginning, rather than waiting until the end.

24

I awaken at sea, and find myself watching a girl who has awakened with no memory. They tell me that she has gone insane and killed many. She asks why they aren't trying to kill her. The sailors say she is their daughter and they want her to work for them.

25

I find myself in a far away land, trying to win back the heart of a girl I lost long ago. I follow her deep into the woods and travel upstream to a lake. I see bears and eventually find these lizard creatures in the water. I am on an Island in the center of the lake, the creatures surround me. They have tails with stingers at the end. I enter the water, and as they chase me to shore they sting me and their stingers are like fire.

26

I stand on a cliff overlooking the ocean. There is a small bay beneath me with a rocky coast shore. There are two women below. I have not been here in thousands of years. We had been in the forest, when something happened: there was a surge of some kind – a flash of light, and we were pushed to this time. I find a staircase leading down to the sea. I descend. Once there I communicate with the women; there is some debate over whether or not I will be able to function sexually with them.

FLASH. I am now alone with this girl who is supposed to be my daughter, but somehow is not. We are at a ballpark. The chain link fence and green field behind are the setting.

We are speaking. I believe I say something to the effect of,
"I see what is inside the mind. Some people only see the outside and make decisions to cast out based on [*because of*] appearance, but I see [*hear*] that which is within [*the heart*]."

She is a creature who I have not known before. She has tiger stripes and her eyes are bright. She begins to glow and her shape is shifting before my eyes, as she explains how she changes color. I have the impression that she is a shape shifter struggling with rejection. We part ways. I don't know why.

FLASH. I have sudden memory of a man driving me around everywhere. When we return to the parking lot in the forest where our journey began, I understand. The man touring me around is an important man, with a busy schedule and driver of his own. He has taken the time to teach me.

I hear the words echoing inside my mind,

"*The master is not above the servant; nor the servant above the master.*"

But, beloved, be not ignorant
of this one thing, that one day
is with the Lord as a thousand
years, and a thousand years as
one day.

2 Peter 3:8

David Burton

CHAPTER SEVEN

I give myself to God.

🌿 **2** 🌿

I am in a cavern beneath the earth; people have gathered around me. I am trying to tell them the truth of their situation, but many are deceived by a man. I am playing guitar and I begin to play the song that is inside my heart. I decide to lead the people and the girl I am with out of darkness, and into freedom.

The man does not want me to do this. He does everything in his power to fight against me, but to no avail. I have compassion and allow him to live, rather than destroying his existence. In frustration he torches the cavern, enveloping it in flames. I lead the people down a small passageway, toward a door, but the evil pursues us. I open the hatch and send the girl I love through into the daylight. I follow.

FLASH. We run down a series of embankments, each one with a road dividing it. We run away from the evil that pursues us.

FLASH. I stand in a circular clearing like a field, surrounded by an embankment. On the ledge I can see a house burning in the distance. A man emerges from the burning building and approaches the edge of the clearing. I walk toward him and confront him. He says that he was used, and did not orchestrate anything. I tell him to grow plants and never get involved again, otherwise I will kill him. He walks away.

FLASH. I am in traffic when people with weapons surround several cars and begin taking people away. Their leader is the man I let live in that dark cavern. I am angry. I try to hide my face, but someone singles me out. I stand from my place of hiding, revealing myself to the enemy, and attack. I walk quickly toward him, but stop several paces away.

I warn him of his coming death by my hand. From then on, I and this girl beside me hunt him with the sole purpose of ending his life. **FLASH**. I am with her at school; I fall in love. I want to be with her forever. We are in class working on algebraic equations. I leave the class and go to save another girl from the wreckage of a car. We end up sleeping together.

3

The world is being flooded. I knew it would come. I see the water and mud pouring into the valley. I get into a vehicle and seek higher ground. She is going to meet me and we are leaving. We finally find each other, but it is much later. We are together, she is sculpting, and the sculpture is covered in a white shirt. I hold her in my arms.

4

I hunt a murderer who is able to shift shape into woodland creatures. I find several watches that belong now only to the dead.

5

I am in a city and it is summer. The grass has turned brown and the nights have turned warm. I wait for her near the fence; eventually she comes, but we need blankets.

FLASH. I am in the forest. I need to walk to the end of the road in darkness to meet the dealer. I arrive at the top of the road only to find he is in the nearby hotel. I walk quickly and enter the room. He is there with several others. He has tattoos of black feathers all over his arms and he speaks with a musical, clear and confident voice. I am impressed and he gives me more rock than I could imagine. I leave and throw it in the pipe right away. Blast. Load. Blast. Load.

FLASH. I am in a vehicle, driving somewhere; a girl and I are in the back, smoking rock without a pipe that works. I keep inhaling but not getting enough. Suddenly everything goes wrong. The car crashes, the driver murders the girl and tries to hide the weapon. It is a vacant lot next to an old broken crumbling building. Concrete and plastic is scattered all throughout the patches of green grass. I

David Burton

find the man, disarm him, and I am about to end him when my heart breaks because I discover it is my father.

FLASH. I am in a garage bay trying to fix the chain that holds open the door. It hasn't worked in years.

6

I am in a hotel room with several other people. I hate them. There is liquor everywhere and everyone is having sex. It's all twisted and weird. Finally, some people leave and I follow them out the door. I walk to another room on the third floor. It is better than the last, even with all the blood red cloth and curtains draped over everything.

7

I am in the darkness talking to a white skull with cords running off it in all directions. It is connected to the ceiling. It wants to come out; it wants to be free. Powers will not allow it. There are several creatures that I do not understand; yet, I am drawn to them. I want to know them. I see a glimpse of the truth, and *for a moment* I *see* — eyes burning bright in the blackness of night. A flash and it is gone, replaced by the world I have come to know. The war is being fought one battle at a time.

FLASH. I find three women living on a farm in the valley. A dirt path leads to their house, which I follow. They know who I am and offer encouragement. These three could very possibly be *the* three from long ago.

8

I stand in the sand, near the ocean, facing a demon. I have fallen in love with his daughter, and we are trying to escape his reach. I am about to engage in warfare when I *hear* a call, and I must leave. A stone archway appears behind me, with a gateway standing open at the top of the steps. A piece of my armour is in another world, hidden beneath a stone, and I must retrieve it.

"Do not even *try* to rise against me," I say to the demon as I turn, ascend the stone path, and walk through the gate.

꼭 **9** 꼭

This story begins long ago, in a gathering many people attended. It is where I met her for the first time. We were drawn to each other, and before long we were walking alone. I stood there, staring into her eyes, wanting her touch, her skin against mine, and to know who she is. When I left the gathering, she followed.

FLASH. I enter another building with the girl, finding several friends waiting within. These are the people who I have trusted at some point in some way. They have come to witness us join in eternal union. The room is square with a single archway standing at each side.

We are married near a doorway with people on either side. I don't understand exactly why we marry, but there is a voice within my mind and a presence in my heart that tells me she is the right girl. That no matter the circumstance I will always love her; and that one day, she may love me in return. I begin to understand that I have married a stranger, and that she has done so for a reason unknown. I stare into her eyes as we slide further apart. I know what is about to happen, yet I love her anyway.

The room begins to change as the four arch doorways shift, closing and opening. The room has moved and now resides in a new building in a new world. Women dressed as nurses are opening the doors and entering the room. The girl is taken from me. I am left alone inside the empty room, but within my mind a vision begins to play.

I see where she has been taken. She enters a room where several men are seated around a table. They tell her that she has completed her task by marrying me, and that the information they need will soon be in their hands. I see the rage building inside her and watch as she suddenly snaps. Her heart has changed. She walks to the table and removes several battery type objects from a system and leaves. They have no choice; she has all the power because she has me.

She enters the empty room where I stand, and beckons for me to follow her. Knowing what has transpired, I quickly fall in step behind her. She leads me to another room where we use technology unlike anything here. Two chairs stand alone inside the room. I sit in one, and she in the other.

She explains quickly how the system operates. Visualize in your mind and the object will appear holographically in front of you in the air. I concentrate and demonstrate my ability. The process is easy, as if I was designed for it.

They want to know about the ship: a certain section of it near the engines. I create the image, rotate it and try to disappear it; next, I create myself staring out of the mirror.

FLASH. In the long ancient past, a woman loved a man who became a ship. He turned evil and would not listen to his first love – her. He became more and more so, until one day he set off to destroy worlds. Instead, she destroyed him, but it cost her. She fell through the clouds, landing on a spear, blood spilling upon the ground.

FLASH. They granted the power to one long ago and it ended in the death of many of their own kind. I understand the hesitation of granting the power to anyone again.

FLASH. We are walking, the girl and I, in winter along the side of a city street. I hold her hand. I ask her,

"Now that I know why we came together do you want to remain?"

"No," she says.

"Why?" I ask. "Can't you see I love you?"

Doesn't she understand that nothing in her past will stop me or keep me from loving her with all my heart, and that I see her for who she really is. We turn and enter a vehicle; we must go somewhere. The road is very difficult as obstacles keep coming, like tires rolling off a truck flat bed. She is a skilled driver and fighter; I am impressed and I love her more because now that I know she is *with* me. It can't be hidden.

"They are trying to kill us." I say as we escape into darkness.

FLASH. We sit across from each other at a table, a friend is with her. Her friend is asking her why she has done this and how it is possible. I look up into their eyes and respond. *All* our eyes are on fire and I sense surprise. I was not supposed to hear the question.

"Because God is with me." I gesture to my right.

"Because I know, and have always known, what it coming." I sense something. "You may not be able to see at the moment, but one day you will understand."

I project love, looking into her eyes as I awake.

For ye were sometimes
darkness, but now are ye light
in the Lord: walk as children
of light.

Ephesians 5:8

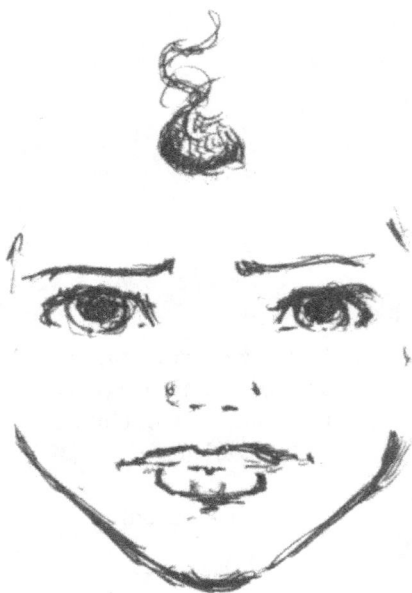

David Burton

CHAPTER EIGHT

I am on the sand in the predawn daylight; the tide is out and the ship is just beyond it. The waves are crashing on the shore. A man is with me, deciding whether to sail. He decides and I run down the sand, calling the sailors. People appear out of strange places.

2

I stand in a wizard's house, staring at the walls. I know that something lay hidden within. I touch a segment of the wall, and a secret compartment opens, revealing a sword and a bow.

3

There is a machine which creates a time snake, a portal which travels between worlds. Within each cube, it does not require the eighth segment. Someone else was monitoring the signal and trying to use it to see us, eventually to take the program.

FLASH. I see my father and we talk about the dead. I see images of people I know laying on the shore of a sea, with water lapping up over their heads. It is strange.

FLASH. I am in a car driving down a highway, but I'm not driving. I tell the driver to pull over. I get out of the car and see that it is missing several parts. I walk to the junkyard and ask about the pieces I need. The man says he does not have anything I require.

FLASH. The girl I have chosen to love finds me doing something wrong. She leaves, angry. I turn, cross the street, walk down an alley and into darkness. I run toward the wall and bounce. The anger and dark fury twisting within me becomes unleashed, spiraling and kindling the spark that will soon burst into flame.

❧ 4 ☙

There is war. I have landed on the beach and I am waiting for the flight crew to arrive with my aircraft. There is a battle raging within the city but it is unclear as to who exactly it is that we fight against.

FLASH. I stand on the shore of the ocean. I feel different. A craft of some sort has crashed here and we are left to survive, but many of the people having forgotten how to live off the land. People are fighting on the sand about a fish hook. It appears that one girl has taken it. I feel compassion and walk into the water. I reach down and touch the water: I am calling the fish.

❧ 5 ☙

I am walking through the forest with other people when the person in front of me disappears. I turn, walk backward and run into a girl. She is beautiful and I ask where this pathway goes to. I follow her to a house. Then I turn and walk the path alone. I find an abandoned guitar. I search to the left, the right, and finally enter the room in front of me.

FLASH. I am in a city far away. I think it is New York. I am walking around with my guitar and someone else is with me. He is walking ahead of me. We are in a train station where I meet a pretty girl. I ask her where the worst part of town is because I want to go there. Then I sit with her and play guitar. At first it is difficult to concentrate and get the chords to work properly. Soon, I play reasonably, but not great. I have a hard time keeping the rhythm.

Somewhere within this dream I see a huge churning cloud with fire bursting upward from the earth into the sky.

❧ 6 ☙

I am standing in a circular room with several doors. Through one door is a girl. I enter her room. I kiss her and I am aroused because she is sexy. She tells me she won't have sex with me at the moment, but she says she can turn over and masturbate. I say sure. There are glass windows all around me, with the sun burning bright in the sky on the other side.

FLASH. I stand in the circular room again with the walls made out of glass. It is sunset. I walk outside. There is a lake and a small dock. I feel the presence of evil. I can sense it. I see a cat floating by as though an invisible entity is holding it in their hand. I turn and run, saying,

"In the name of our Lord and Saviour Jesus Christ, I cast thee out." My speech is slow. I say it several times and awake.

I look around at the darkness, considering whether I should go back and fight. I decide, close my eyes and return.

I am standing at the entrance to the glass circular room. I walk forward onto the walkway and descend the stairs. I see a trail of smoke moving and twisting above the flames. I sense the presence of something. It is familiar, yet strange. I cast it out again, angry that I had to come back and still find it present, yet hidden.

"In the name of our Lord and Saviour Jesus Christ, I cast thee out." I stutter and then awake to the darkness of my room. I yell the words again into the night and consider why this is occurring. I reflect upon every open book and object in my room. I close my eyes and return to the world.

I return to a different place, a far away city. I walk the streets of the city toward a place I know by instinct. I don't know how, I just have an intrinsic knowledge of the place. When I arrive there is a black man at the gate – we are friends, of a kind. He asks what I have to trade. Not much, I reply; soon, I will. I turn and walk back toward my land.

As I walk a girl approaches me, asking,
"Do you want anything?" Her voice is sweet, seductive yet innocent.

"No," I reply.

"Do you want to come to my house?" She asks.

"I don't have any drugs."

She parts her blouse and says, "No, me." She is offering herself.

"No," I say as I turn and walk away.

This is when *she* sees me and reveals her presence. She is pleased. She is dressed in rags, and standing behind a line drawn in the sand. I cross over the line and we are suddenly in a palace. She is in my arms. I hold her close and tight against me. A man offers us two cigarettes. The scene shifts around me and she is gone.

FLASH. I am in a library or study with a person who is asking me questions. Books line the shelves. He speaks. I do not listen. "I have a wife and children. Do you understand?" Then I get angry and leave. I may have wrecked the office as I left.

FLASH. I am in a chair on the dock. I see several houses floating upon the water and I am given the reassurance that all is well. Those who were meant to come together have come together and formed a community. A little girl comes to me and climbs into my lap. We are talking. She is my daughter? She talks to me and I ask her how old she is.

FLASH. Two creatures appear that are very strange; they emerge from the water and climb onto the dock. I don't know much of what is happening here. One perhaps helps me and then returns to the water from which they came and swim away.

❧ 7 ☙

I return from a far journey. I go to a room within a building that stands in a city. As I get into bed, a blonde girl comes into the room and asks why I am here. I tell her I've been clean for a long time and I am here to go back to work. She is happy and we got to a meeting. No one is surprised to see me. Someone asks why I am there; I say I am ready to work. After the meeting the woman tells me that if I want to work here I must live here, then she takes me into the room.

FLASH. I leave and return with my robot, who is in need of repair. The girl shows me where I must take him. The man takes apart the robot before I can say anything. I am pissed right the fuck off. He reassembles him but this guy is an idiot and he fucks it up. He ends up destroying my robot friend. The girl tells me I must return the robot and I freak out. I turn on the robot and discover that he is completely changed: he has been destroyed. I am sad. I leave, far away.

FLASH. Someone is chasing me; so I leave and go to another world.

FLASH. My father searches for me and asks me to return. I appear to him for a moment. He asks what I am doing.

"Abstract architecture," I reply. I hold up a misshapen rectangular piece of wood. "We could cut this, *corner to corner*." We both say at the same time. He smiles and I get the sense he understands, even more than I. There is a gateway of blue light behind me which I turn and step back through.

❧ 8 ☙

I am in school. There is a beautiful girl near me. I have no idea how we end up together, but we do. And I am very satisfied. I am outside with her on the green grass behind a baseball diamond. I take her hand in mine; we are connected. She begins to understand that. I want her – love her – for who she is, no matter what. And this is when things become strange. We enter a classroom or church in a building. The girl tells me I have mail. I reach into her backpack and pull out an envelope. I open it and find a bill from something long ago in a different city. The girl leaves and I make a choice to go with her because that is what I promised her.

FLASH. I am outside sleeping on the ground. I awake – it is night. I see a silhouette of a building and rooftop edge. There is a figure sitting on the peak. I run toward the building and leap into the sky. My first attempt falls short and I sense their laughter. I perceive that there are two figures on the peak. I run, leap and land on the peak directly between the two figures. I sense their surprise. I know they are here to hurt or somehow damage the girl I love. The one on the left is wolfen and the one on the right is vampiric. I reach out and place a hand on each and take a handful: then I leap in to the air, taking them with me – I spin forward and slam them upon the ground, destroying both of them.

FLASH. I've entered "the tree" in which is a vine structure that people are climbing up and down; not many seem to be able to reach the top: it appears that they are *not aware* of the opening at the top of the tree. So, many enter at the center gate and end up dropping into the chasm. I warn them to get out of my way, *kindly*. I spin, drop and land before the center gate. I walk out into the sunlight of the park beach harbour. The point curves out to the right. I'm running in the sand. My ship is out there somewhere. It is unseen but I am not disturbed because I can feel its presence.

I come to the edge of the point and find the base of a cliff. There is an opening out of which pours a river that feeds into the sea. There is a doorway beside the stream, out of which I can hear the voice of a girl from my past. I am close. I can't remember the words. I enter the doorway and climb a flight of stairs. She is standing at the top, clear as day.

"I'm here," I say. She looks at me, confused and surprised. She doesn't voice it, but I get the impression that part of her thinks I should be elsewhere. "Do you know who I am? Are you able to recognize me?" She squinches her face in concentration, her blue eyes glassy.

"No," she replies. I remove the sunglasses I am wearing and stare into her blue eyes. I project something: security, assurance. The glass door inside the glass wall behind her opens and we walk within the inner room. A male presence is in the room. He is in charge of this world, in a way. At first he is firm, angry yet graceful. He says nothing, yet I know he waits for an explanation.

"I'm late." He is curious; how do I know what is happening. "I had to make a phone call." We argue non-verbally until I come to the sensory conclusion that he is happy that I am here, as I belong –

David Burton

even if it has taken some time. Time appears to be of no concern to him.

❦ 9 ❦

I find someone smuggling children into a steel gray aluminum workshop. They are in bonds with bits in their mouth. The man does not speak English. I tell the person he must let me see the child. I soon discover that he has many of these children. I travel, where another girl, one from my past, comes with us. She is aroused and is all over me, in love with me. It seems very good to me; yet somehow, something goes wrong.

FLASH. I walk out of a passageway [*gateway*] onto a beach of sand that stretches to the mountains. There are stone pillars arranged in a semi-circle, close nearby.

"I know this place." There is a circle in which I'm standing. I stretch my arms out slightly to each side, palms down and *lift* – I'm in the air, as though not a single day has passed. The one who is with me does not seem impressed, so I use my mind, less action with my hands and raise quickly into the sky. I come down, hovering above the ground. "I can feel a solid beneath the palms of my hands." I get no response. I can feel the ocean and hear its waves pounding.

FLASH. I am back inside the gray building talking to the man about some of his children, we are discussing some of the problems he has been having. I ask him how angry they are. A car approaches the door. I spin and turn through the door as an object comes out of the vehicle's window, falling into the house. The explosion pushes the aluminum siding out. I can feel the force of an air concussion.

I walk back into the building, searching for survivors. The children are hurt, bleeding. I become angry. I run after the vehicle and torch it; as soon as I spark the flame, I realize they are also children. I stop the vehicle and pull the occupants into daylight and safety. I am crying.

FLASH. A woman in a trench coat is approaching me, saying: "We are going on the road again." I take her in my arms and hold her

Wall Between Worlds

tight. I whisper into her ear, through her blonde hair, "You aren't going."

❦ 10 ❧

I am in a building, talking to a man who knows many things. I am talking to him about technology. A silence descends over the building and I know something is amiss. I run to the window and look out. I look up and down the street. The vehicles are out front and everything looks okay, except that there are no people anywhere. I turn and look to the right, just in time to see a helicopter drop an object with a blue glow before disappearing around the corner.

I turn, grab hold of the man and run toward the stairs. The man understands immediately. I am with my family: father, mother, and sister. And yet they are not my family. I lead them to the basement as we run. The doors to the basement are smoking. I smash the fire glass on the wall and pull out the hose, or extinguisher. It is only the seams of the door that are smoldering and I realize we have been set up. There is no fire here, only a distraction to keep us from moving onward. There is not much time left. I push open the door, run down the stairs, and burst into a room. Too much glass. I seek concrete. The liquid blue fire is coming and the air concussion will likely collapse the building.

We continue through another room and into what appears to be a parking garage. We find cover. The fire comes. I prepare myself to have the flesh burned off me, but I am shielded, protected. The building begins to collapse and I pull my mother out of the path of destruction. The collapse kills the other half of my family.

"Why didn't they keep their eyes open!?" I scream in futility.

"Because people respond this way. They close their eyes and hope it will be alright. There is nothing wrong with this, but sometimes you must have faith and keep your eyes open at the same time."

David Burton

Who said that?

FLASH. I'm in a small restaurant meeting. There is a man on the stage talking into the microphone about destruction or something. He speaks of things he does not know or understand. I lose it. My family is dead. I walk to the front, take the microphone and walk outside. I sit in the dying rays of the sun as it falls beneath the horizon. I speak into the microphone, speaking the truth of my experience, and then I explain that it is the man at the front who has caused this horrible thing. The entire speech is said both in the dream and waking. I remember being awake and within the dream *at the same time.*

FLASH. I am in a cavern. There is writing on the walls. Someone comes in and erases the writing. I am upset. I've been waiting for a girl from my past. She arrives but it is too late: the writing is gone. She loves me anyway.

❧ 11 ❧

I'm on a platform at the base of a set of stairs; there is a computer system that functions as the front desk. I'm trying to figure it out when a beautiful girl comes over and takes interest in what I am searching for. Her hair is long and flowing, her eyes are intense and reflective, but she hides them. We talk and she accepts my invitation to visit the library or I accept hers.

We arrive at the building and select a place to sit. I can feel her touch upon me. A couple of men try to harass the girl I am with. There are strange burns on their skin – the surface is bubbling and infected. It moves as if alive, breathing. I feel disgusted. She is angry: these are her enemies of a sort. She freaks out when one of their burns bursts and explodes infection all across the clothes she wears.

I also have a burn, but the skin is healthy and peeling; beneath the flaking white skin is a tattoo of a green blue planet.

FLASH. I am on a playing field, hovering above the ground, yet not in complete control of flight. It is being altered by a presence on the field. I search it out and change something.

✤ 12 ✤

I dream of a sword coming from a wall, and a train, which I missed.

FLASH. I am in a room. The cats crawl in my sleeves: they jump to the shelf above me.

FLASH. White dress, black dress, white dress, red dress: white thong. See through material.

FLASH. A broken stereo behind me; a broken stairwell before me. People who don't belong; missing the one who should be here. I leave and work for a security company of some kind, but it's all a front for something else.

FLASH. I stand in a dark room, staring at the blue eyes glowing in the darkness.

We speak without a sound.

✤ 13 ✤

It all started with the rock. I drove to the mall and left the car to go shopping. People kept giving me money. I had a stack of twenty dollar bills in my back pocket, and the dealer appears at my side. I buy a hundred worth. I thank him and he disappears. I walk into the store and reach into my pocket to make sure it's still there. When I pull it out into my hand it falls to the floor and bounces. I reach quickly and pick it up as it is still rebounding; this happens twice, so I put the rock inside my mouth. When I get to the sandwich counter I take it out and wrap it in saran. The store is closing.

FLASH. I am in a house. It is painted white. I've been here before, a long time ago, but the house looked different then. It had a division down the middle and it was dark and aging. The outside used to be as a cabin in the forest; now, it has been developed and landscaped. There are people near me, and I want them gone.

FLASH. I am looking inside a room, where a computer system is running. I look back into the inner room. It looks empty, but I feel a presence and something is off-key.

FLASH. I am outside in an open air barn with the animals. There are young cattle. I am communicating with them. They accept me. There is an older beast in the next stall. I try to communicate, but it is pissed off about my presence and continuously attempts to exert his leadership of the herd. I try to explain that I am just a visitor [*a healer*] here only for a short time, yet the whole earth is mine and for me.

FLASH. There are a few people trying to watch or listen to a device. I move to the center of the room and tell them that I am the antenna.

FLASH. I am out back the building, looking at the field next to me. I see a girl come out and walk around. As she comes closer I see she is dressed in a strange costume, like an actress on stilts, a performer. She drops and is normal height, standing before me. She rolls backward, exposing her vagina to me in the process.

At first it is exhilarating and I am aroused. Then I see the black edges of infection and skin death around her labia. She completes the roll and is standing before me. She is blonde and incredibly beautiful. Her eyes are like star bursts that have lost their initial fire, but remain burning, glowing like the embers of coal in a dying fire.

I ask for her number so that we can get together and have sex. I know that she is with sickness, but I am absolutely certain that I will not be infected through contact; in fact, I will probably have a positive impact on everything in her life. I'm still aroused.

14

The girl I'm with has killed someone and brought me the meat harvested from the body. I marinade it with sugar and ginger. Something goes wrong; people come to our place and start asking questions – one of them takes my wife into the next room. I hear her telling the person that I killed her mother – not true. She did it and now she is setting me up.

"Do you think I will be home by tonight?" I ask my friends.

They say *yes* with their mouth and *not likely* with their mind. I flee. I circle around the building, duck down an alley and into a field. It is hot, off goes my shirt. I see a path on a hillside leading into the forest. I follow it, but in the first tree line, while still on the hillside, I hear the blades of a helicopter slicing the air. I climb the tree, attempting to hide. I see a man crossing the field and I know they have found me.

I run toward the man and as he attempts to seize me I use his own strength against him, throwing him to the ground. I catch him before he lands and place him gently upon the earth.

Just because I can overpower these earth creatures does not mean I should harm them. They don't know what they are doing.

The second man tries and I do the same. Now, three attempt at once. Two aim for the lower body while one takes my arm. He tries to pull it out of joint.

"What the fuck is your problem?" I ask him. I can sense the evil of his nature.

FLASH. I am outside of an aquatic center; it is winter. Someone is coming for me, and she has taken the penguins. When she finds me she says,

"The center is cut out of the ice and the platform collapsing : the water rising – the center, sinking."

13 In thoughts from the visions of the night, when deep sleep falleth on men,

14 Fear came upon me, and trembling, which made all my bones to shake.

15 Then a spirit passed before my face; the hair of my flesh stood up:

16 It stood still, but I could not discern the form thereof: an image was before mine eyes, there was silence, and I heard a voice, saying,

Job 4

David Burton

CHAPTER NINE

This all begins in darkness. I stand in the sand beside the ocean. An evil presence comes and reveals itself, but I cast it far away. There is light burning in the dark. I look in its direction and the see the shore engulfed in flames. The fire burns in the sand, and across the water, reaching even to the mountains of distant islands.

Then the vision comes.

I am in the forest, between two nations. The nations are at a time of peace. A young girl grows up within the culture. She is beautiful in body, mind, and soul. One day while she gathers water from a nearby stream, the nations begin to war against each other once again. She comes to me in tears. Her entire family has been killed and her way of life destroyed; her village is gone, and none remain. She asks me why God has chosen to spare her when all the others are dead. I hold her in my arms, look into her blue green eyes, and reply:

"While you were going from person to person, you learned all you could of each one. God has spared you because *you are your people.* All that they were is contained within you."

I leave the girl within the confines of the wood and go to the cities. I must put this war to an end before it gets out of control. I go to each and get them to agree to cease fire; however, while I am in one city, the other fires upon it. Some sort of sound weapon which crumbles the inner city, reducing it to broken stone. I have been given a staff, and when I witness the cunning destruction I become furious. I walk to the city which contains the weapon, raise my staff, and destroy it. Never again will it harm a living soul; not while I remain.

~❧ **2** ☙~

The enemy is coming. I am walking quickly through the grass, down a path that I prepared earlier. The pathway ends at the edge of a cliff. I stand on the edge, staring at the water and stones far below.

The ocean is gray near the base of the cliff, but clear blue further out to sea.

Soldiers are landing on a strip of sand behind me, and I know I must act. I am exposed, standing in the grass. There is no other path open to me, so I look down at the sea and consider the jump. The stones buried beneath the crashing waves cause me to hesitate. There is not much room for error, and I can't establish the depth of the water from this height. I see a man and woman, soldiers, wading near a sandy beach.

I make a decision, leap from the ledge. I fall through the sky, and come crashing into the water, sliding off the side of a stone. I swim toward the sand, walk silently out of the water, and embrace the woman who is waiting for me. The soldiers in the water see us, and come to investigate.

"Why are you here?" They ask.

"We are travelers from another land," we say. "We recently sailed to this land, and discovered the war. We have nothing to do with the current conflict."

The soldiers believe our story, and leave us in peace. As night falls across the earth, we swim out into the ocean, trying to reach our ship. The moment we board the vessel, we pull anchor and drop sail. The wind catches our sail, and we are flying across the waves, but our exhilaration is upset by the sound of jet engines, and wings roaring through the air.

We are caught, suffering the consequences of a war we neither started, nor fight for the moment. We abandon the vessel, and make our way back to the shore, attempting to conceal our presence. The female soldier makes contact with us again. I sense her understanding of our situation.

"I don't know if I will be able to keep your existence hidden from them, even after giving them this information," she says. Her eyes are a bright reflective blue.

David Burton

FLASH. I am in the forest. There is a race being run by the soldiers that have landed on the earth, but they will not allow me to run in the race, and have removed me from it. I refuse to be excluded, so I begin to run.

The soldier leading the race must be destroyed. There is an evil within him, and he is leading the entire group astray. He is not the only obstacle, but my mind is centered in tactics, and I spring into action. My first attack is the lead soldier. He falls into the plant life on the side of the pathway, rolls down an embankment, and lays face down near the water's edge. He could be unconscious, but I think he is dead. I do not hesitate in my decision, quickly eliminating several others from the race.

My tactics are complete, and I walk in silence toward a forest at the edge of the beach. As I pass a stairway made of stone, several people emerge, and confront me. They are angry with my choice, and my attack of the lead runner.

"Why have you done this?" They ask with condemnation in their eyes.

"You do not understand. He is not who he appears to be. He has deceived you all, and is leading you into utter ruin. He was never supposed to be here, but you have fallen for the lie, and welcomed into your arms."

The woman is at my side again, and she stands with me in faith against that opposition that tries to condemn us. Although our enemy seeks to imprison us, we are freed by our allegiance to our country, and our way of life.

FLASH. A woman having sex, covered in blood; blood pouring from her – she rides the man, tries to stand and passes out.

❦ **3** ❦

I am standing at the edge of the city, where the forest begins. A man has stopped me, and is asking about several things. We look at the sky. It is a churning cloud, burning bright with light. He asks, we say,

"He is coming. The master comes." We look into each other's eyes, and understand we have found common ground.

"He comes, and all will be destroyed."

❦ 4 ❧

I am walking through the grass with a beautiful girl. The field rests on the top of a cliff – the ocean below, out of sight. She is angry with me, but stays for some strange reason. We are drawn to each other, attracted – we walk through a land of darkness, and emerge out the other side. A pale light has risen in the sky.

❦ 5 ❧

It ends with me waking in the morning, the bright sun shining in the window. A new day is dawning with an amazing blue sky. I go to sleep and awake in darkness, the stars shining brightly in the sky.

"I awoke and it was daylight. Why is it night?"

FLASH. I am outside, screaming at someone sitting on the side of the road, answering a question that I can't remember being asked.

"When you understand that I am the alien and the stranger that is spoken of in the word. I come from above," I say, pointing to the blue sky filled with clouds above me. "I reside here on earth." I am screaming these words.

FLASH. I'm in a vehicle, driving down an old gravel road. We move slowly toward the highway in the distance. It is dark. I am the passenger, and the driver is asking me for directions.

"How do I find the path?" she asks.

"Your light is off," I say. I reach across the steering wheel, and pull the switch. Several things happen all at once. I see the road, she

David Burton

increases her speed, she misses the corner, we slide off the gravel, and drive off an embankment. I feel us leave the ground, and I know we are in the air off the edge of a cliff.

"I love you, God." I know I am to find death.

FLASH. I am in a hallway. It is marble with alternating colors: white, black. There is a doorway at one end of the hall and a stairway at the other. I play a stringed musical instrument. The chording is wrong. I hear where it needs repair, or development. The sun is shining, rays of light pass through the door, spilling onto the floor.

❦ 7 ❦

I awake in a distant land. A land of crops, and scattered farms. I am digging a trench with a shovel. I sense the movement of something in the distance, a darkness. I am wearing a silver ring with a white stone beneath it, pressed against my skin. I walk quickly away from the trench in pursuit of knowledge and understanding.

❦ 8 ❦

I am walking down the street. I notice the house I am walking past is my childhood home. There are several people walking in the early evening, drinking alcohol, making their way to a gathering. They ask me to walk with them.

Soon, we arrive at a house, and we enter. I am consumed with lust, burning with sexual desire, and I take a drink. I blackout immediately. I awake, laying in a bed.

"Where have the women gone?" I ask.

"They left long ago," a man replies.

"I must have fallen asleep," I say quietly. I rise, and leave.

FLASH. As I walk down the street, I notice several people passing on the other side. *She* is with them. I cross the street, and walk with her. Hours pass, and eventually we find ourselves in the depths of a forest. I fall asleep in her arms.

FLASH. I am outside of a house, kicking in the door. I see a man above me in the glass window, covered in blood, and freaking out. I break down the door. The man throws money out the window, trying to cause distraction. I hunt him down as he runs. I catch him, and murder him, with a cold hatred in my heart.

 9

I am walking through a stairwell behind a building which connects two rooms. Inside one of the rooms I see a girl. We begin to communicate and it is awesome. I am kind to her and she is kind to me.

FLASH. We are crossing the ocean together. We grow closer – we are falling in love again. We come to the Island and climb from the water. She asks me about flight. I feel the wind against my skin, I see the stars in the sky. We return to the place where we came from before: it is here that I tell her father that I had an amazing experience.

I keep the truth hidden. I keep the ring and bracelet that is hers. It is a signal to her that I will commit to her, no matter what happens in life. I see her smile quietly out of the corner of my eye. We are standing in a room, changing our clothes. There is a doorway being restored between us at the back of the room – it is black on the other side.

 10

I am standing in front of a house, watching it burn in the darkness. I am outside the fire, but I must enter the blaze. There is something I need to retrieve. I walk through the flames, smash the wall, and enter the building. I am trying to save a stamp, or some other object.

❧ 11 ❧

I'm in a prison, and someone is trying to test chemical weapons inside. I'm surprised. There are dead bodies everywhere. They are releasing a black creature at the far end of the compound. I take one of the vials they are testing and get close enough to pierce the creature. It dies. I leave the prison.

❧ 12 ❧

I spend nearly the entire night talking aloud, waking, sleeping, dreaming – all becomes one. I remember being on the bleachers with several girls. I find a cell phone and an envelope containing five thousand dollars. I return the cell phone and money, accidently to the wrong person. I find the right girl at the end, and I ask her how she made the money.

"Dancing," she says. I tell her I will help get her cell phone back, but not the money because she obtained it by dancing naked and it is the same as prostitution.

FLASH. I have bubble gum in my mouth and each time I pull a piece out, it increases in my mouth. I tear a piece, throw it in the ocean, and repeat the process over and over. The ocean has pink individual gobs of goo that come together to form something I can't see.

❧ 13 ❧

I am standing in the medical laboratories of an underground secret installation. The scientists have decided to clone the genetic content of a dangerous alien creature – one they think they can control.

Several of us know better and we kill the creature's offspring as soon as it is born; its blood soaks our clothing. Now, its scent is upon us. We know the creature will hunt us and seek vengeance.

In transport we hijack the shipping container and bring it to a previously prepared place of containment. We free the creature into a concrete cavern which stretches far beneath the surface of the earth. There is a gateway nearby and a stairway which descends into darkness behind it. I refuse to enter. The people I am with are attempting to set off an explosive device which will destroy the creature. I am unaware of the detonation.

FLASH. I stand before an alien vessel. The first passageway behind the hatch is only a flight deck for the pilot. The inner workings and living quarters are hidden from view and accessible only through voice command. This ship belongs to a different race of alien creatures; one that I know and am a part of in some way. The ship needs an electrical charge to operate, and I attempt to charge the ship.

FLASH. She is with me and we come together sexually to discuss our inner thoughts; our beings meet and talk in a spiritual dimension.

❦ 14 ❧

I awake in a strange bed with white sheets. A girl is laying beside me, a video camera and a porn magazine also lay on the scattered sheets. Her eyes open at the same time as mine; neither of us know where we are, how we got there or what happened the previous night. I grab the camera and hang the strap on my shoulder. We get dressed and go looking for the vehicle, which is down the street at the local pub. We find the keys in the adjacent room. I place the key in the ignition; it turns over, but refuses to start. I unscrew the gas cap and find the tank empty. The girl takes the vehicle across the street and fills the tank. We drive away.

I awake in a strange bed with white sheets. A girl is laying beside me – *I remember the dream*. A video camera is laying beside me. I grab the camera and place the strap around my shoulder. Tiffany is awake; neither of us know where we are, how we got there or what happened the previous night. We agree the camera will reveal some sort of sexual encounter. I take the keys off the counter and fifty cents in change for gas for the vehicle at the local pub. As I walk out the door, a girl comes outside from the house next door. She smiles at me; she has seen me last night and knows something sexual has gone on. She notices the camera and is excited. I find the vehicle, cross the street and fill the gas tank. I drive away.

David Burton

Dreams within dreams.

❧ 15 ❧

I am standing in my small apartment. I load, fire and inhale. I awake holding my breath. I exhale and return. This happens several times in quick succession.

I perceive that I am out of fuel for the drug fire so I walk downtown and attempt to find more. I enter a small night club and have a drink. I can't find what I am looking for. I glance at my watch and see it is two o'clock in the morning. I say to myself, *if only there were a package left in my pocket.* I reach into my jacket and find two packages. I am pleased and return to my apartment.

I load, fire, inhale and awake holding my breath. I exhale and return.

I leave the apartment and open a doorway; behind it is a stairway descending into the earth. I follow it and eventually find others such as myself. There is a fire burning somewhere inside the earth. I return to the surface and awake.

FLASH. I stand in bleachers of a gathering. People are discussing many things; they are looking for hope and a reason to continue.

FLASH. I am outside the complex and an explosion rocks the foundation. Something has happened. I follow a trail of water into the far reaches of the complex. I find a hidden passageway that functions as an escape route. I find a message in a book. I tell the woman standing at the opening that she must blast the passageway and fill it with rock so it can never be used again. She does not understand, but I tell her she must do this.

❧ 16 ❧

I am standing on a mountain, but I am seeing everything that is happening far away. I see two girls in this vision. They know of my journey, and are planning a surprise sex party when I return. Only they are at the base of the wrong mountain, another mountain with the same name. I see them undressing, one behind the other.

❧ 17 ❧

I am in another city; I am a playwright. I attend part of the play but leave early because I have to talk to someone in a different section of the city. I travel a road and end up at a building near the ocean. I look out over the water and can see the mountains in the distance, covered with snow. I enter through the door and talk to the woman at the front desk. I ask about the ferry and she tells me there is a free ferry. I follow the hallway and find a display about polar bears. I am confused. I return to the desk. She tells me that she knew I had misunderstood and that the ferry is for old people and others travelling to a different destination.

FLASH. I am standing outside the hall where my play has been performed. It is over and they are closing the doors. I run up the steps and say to the man,

"I am the playwright. After the play I am supposed to receive a percentage of ticket sales. Without the money I can't catch the ferry and return to the Island."

"Hold on," he says and disappears behind the glass. He returns with money and steps outside to have a cigarette before walking home.

"It was a good play, you write well," he says, before asking: "Have you ever met people like your characters?"

❧ 18 ❧

I am standing on the deck of a ship about to set sail, but there is a discussion that disturbs me, and I attempt to leave the ship.

FLASH. I am in a far away land, beyond the reach of the world. I am inside a house and I know she is near – I can feel her presence. I walk outside onto a platform; there is a barren land before me, a small patch of green plant life off in the distance. I walk toward the grass, and along the way I see people building an engine: two parallel turbines which push air toward one side.

I see her, but I do not approach. I feel the wind begin to blow, and lean back into it until I am suspended in the air. I feel alive. I drift and come near the edge of a cliff. I am unafraid because I know the wind will carry me. I am upon the green land now.

19

I am working on a cliff side, excavating the dirt away from the stone, exposing a riverbed. I am near the bottom of the work area. I push once and the last segment of dirt collapses, falling away. I fall over the edge. There is nothing beneath me; I fall, reaching out for tree branches or roots as I fall. I find myself falling through a forest of interwoven logs. They begin collapsing and falling past me. I barely avoid them.

They crash into the ocean below. This fall takes a very long time. I finally plunge into the water, as more logs slam down around me, sending spray up the cliff side and raising the water level. I am shocked. I swim to shore and walk up the staircase which is now hidden under water. A girl comes out to meet me; she is concerned.

FLASH. I am standing on the rock shore; huge stones lead out into the wave crashing ocean. A girl goes before me and another wizard. I dance from rock to rock without missing a step. I pass them and slide into the water. I lay there on the shore as waves come up over my body.

There is a house on the shore. The girl comes to me, takes my hand and we stand together. I love her, completely. We walk back up the rock path. She falls, but I catch her in my arms.

"I will always catch you when you fall." She looks at me, her eyes glow with intensity, sadness (on the verge of tears) and love – undying, unending love.

FLASH. We are standing in a swamp, investigating strange objects and equipment. We are searching for a body, but find none until I point at an object (like a canvas sack) with a number on it, bobbing in the water.

"The buoy?" A person beside me asks.

"That is not a buoy, it is a body." I reply. As I walk toward it, it sinks into the water and disappears. I search, but find nothing. It resurfaces behind me. We tear open the canvas and find a uniformed robotic man. The people I am with do not understand, nor comprehend what is happening.

I am given a vision – [FLASH] – People in a laboratory building these robots, modeling them after themselves – [FLASH] – I am on a flight out over the raging sea; we are approaching an ocean platform, a docking bay for ships and helicopters that land upon the water.

One ship is sinking – it has crashed. We land and I run through the corridors of the platform. I burst out through the final door and run quickly to the sinking ship.

"What are you doing!?" I scream at the man who is still in the ship, trying to retrieve a lost item. "Your mother thinks you are dead. Come with me."

He hesitates and then follows me. I tell him I know about the work he is doing, but he must leave with me because the people he works for do not care about him, they only care about the money.

FLASH. I watch as the person I saved walks through a set of doors, followed by his employer. He is saying, "When I said you could see my mother, I did not mean sleep with her." At the same time he realizes that the man has paid his debt.

⚜ **20** ⚜

I look into the sky and see the stars; they are moving. I know what they truly are. I follow the stars; they burn bright for a moment like they have touched the atmosphere briefly. The skies soon cloud over.

FLASH. I am standing in a far away land. Several things happen:

a.   I am given a cloak that glows, shines brightly – it is the sum of all colors, designed.

b.   I am shown how to become transparent, invisible.

FLASH. I am in a city, standing in a room within the forest. There is a bed and a wooden door in the wall. A young blonde girl consumed with sexuality enters the room and climbs into bed with me. My hands explore her body and she is wet between her legs. We are naked and I slip inside her.

Quietly, the door opens and several people are standing in the darkness at the foot of the bed; she senses them and stops sex, breaking contact.

"There are people here," she says.

"They are not," I say.

We both look at the same time: they are gone, but the door remains open. I say, "They are just messing with our minds." She is taken by the thought; her eyes glaze over, and she walks naked through the door, which closes behind her.

FLASH. The people have moved to another section of the forest. They stand in a line, waiting to claim their homes. I leave the line and the girls in it. I will have them later. I move through the wooden stairways, searching. Finally, someone challenges me and we fight. It is horrible; I am disgusted. I murder the man, then I send white gold and a watch to his family, so that they will have money to survive after his death. I weep for the injustice I have committed.

❧ 21 ☙

I am standing in a field, looking out over a small stream into another field with a forest on the far side of the golden wheat grass. I see a fire burning in a small section. I run toward it only to find it has stopped burning by the time I get there. I look back and see it has gone underground and crossed the stream. Small flames leap from the ground, defiantly. I cross back over the water and the flames disappear. I turn around to look at where the fire was to begin with and see a large creature entering the field near the edge of the forest. It is gray, striped in markings like a tiger around its face and chest. I am awed and feared, yet in love with it simultaneously. It comes near me and we communicate.

FLASH. We are standing on the deck of a gray ship, in a dark world. A helicopter is attempting to land to retrieve one of the women.

~ 22 ~

I am standing outside a house in a distant world; the sky is torn with color. I stand in awe and attempt to touch the one I am with, saying, "Look in front of us: see the sun, glowing brightly?" I turn and say, "Now look behind us, see another sun, glowing dimly? See how the night is divided from the day." Something rises inside me. "Look at the other stars [*planets*]. I count five."

FLASH. I am in a room with a girl. She is beautiful, sexy, alive – her eyes always so intense. I am falling in love with her. I hold her in my arms, close to my heart. I remove her clothes while she removes mine. I want to be as close to her as possible; when she touches me I want her to touch my soul, not my skin.

FLASH. I awake within the dream. The entire room has shifted. The dark creatures are here; they stand in front of me. I will not submit. They are going to lose this war. They are testing me, but I remind them that I do not need to speak in order to destroy them.

FLASH. It begins in the distant mountains as a man crosses the plain before the mountain, preparing for his journey. People come to take him away; his wife has been killed. I witness all this happening from a distance. She was writing a book; this man is writing a book. Somehow, the pages interact with each other, and there is a song [*melody*], and message hidden within the text.

FLASH. I am with their daughter. I love her. I am her protector against the darkness that comes for her. I am with her always, and they will never get to her.

David Burton

❧ 23 ❧

I am standing with a girl. I watch as she is reunited with her mother; they are beautiful. The tears begin to flow.

FLASH. I am playing guitar with the same girl; she is rhythm, I am lead. We are in her apartment, but she has not been here for a very long time. I search her shelves for a book I once gave her long ago.

FLASH. I am speaking to a judge about alcoholism and what it is like to not know that you are doing something. I explain about blackout and say if I kill someone it is *negligent homicide*.

FLASH. The architect?

❧ 24 ❧

There is a war raging.

FLASH. I get into my vehicle, like the cockpit of a fighter plane and fly out onto the highway. The vehicle rides on the air and is filled with electronic controls.

FLASH. There is a secret unit of soldiers that are fighting inside a city; a woman works with them. The soldiers are gone one day and she is left alone. She finds weapons and explosives ready to be used, stored in her small cabin. She begins to fear for her life. One day she is coming down the hillside and has a premonition that a train will cross the track. She can't slow down, so she alters something. The train races out across the track, barely missing her and she careens into the side of a house.

FLASH. I am standing near a park shelter. The sky is gray and the rain is falling. I walk inside the shelter. A man approaches and tells me something quickly. I need to remember. People are coming, trying to discover the secret and destroy it. There is a hole in the ground with a steel grate laying on top of it.

I open the cover, removing it from the ground, and I see a liquid deep within. I throw fire into the liquid. I breathe upon it, waiting for it to burst into flames. I see it catch as I run. The explosion rocks the entire world.

FLASH. The world is under attack; something is coming. All the fighter aircraft are destroyed, tossed aside by a powerful wind. I am the last pilot, the only one to get off the launch area. Now, I must stop what is coming.

25

I am in a car, travelling down the road; there is a driver with me. I am searching for a girl who I love. She has been abducted by an evil man. There is little hope in finding the house she has been taken to. We stop at one house that looks familiar to the driver. I exit the vehicle and examine the house. It's not right in some way. A man comes to the window, confused. I ask him if she is here. He says, *no*. I say,

"If I have to come back here and find her in this house I will kill you." I mean every word. We continue the search. I see a house at the end of the street; the door is open. It is the right house, I feel it. I exit the vehicle. The driver hands me a pistol. I take two double-edged blades out of my pocket and place them in my waistband.

I enter the house; he is standing there. I can see the evil in his eyes. I fire two rounds into his body. It does not affect him. I discard the pistol and free the two blades. We fight in close quarters, the blades bounce off his chest plate. He tells me some part of what he has done to the girl. I move in close, drive the blade through his ribs and directly into his heart. He looks at me surprised. I twist the blade and he dies instantly, falling to the floor. The life is gone from his eyes. I free the girl and realize for the first time that his girlfriend is there. I am saddened.

FLASH. The snow is falling, blanketing the field of a farm house out of town. People have gathered and are fighting about something. A man accidently fires an automatic rifle and kills his wife. Security arrives. We all move to the embankment and throw our weapons

David Burton

over the edge. A girl calls to me to get a sample of the snow while I am there. I fill up the vial with the fresh fallen snow and climb up the hill. The snow is very deep.

FLASH. I am downtown after having gone out and left the house. I see several people I know. Most reject me, and one says, "This has to stop at some point," as he walks away from me.

26

I am standing in a hallway. I am fighting an ancient evil: in the appearance of a man. The illusion does not deceive me. I know a name, like others I have known. We are arguing about the state of my soul. He condemns me for the white stone I hold in my hand, projecting that I am bound by it.

"I could regret this later; however, I am no longer in connexion with it."

I toss the stone casually, and seriously out the window.

"In the name of our Lord and Saviour Jesus Christ, I cast thee out."

I awake upon the name of Jesus.

"Fuck you, Satan. Fuck you."

I pray and sleep, only to awaken to another day.

David Burton

I know that thou canst do
every thing, and that no
thought can be witholden
from thee.

Job 42:2

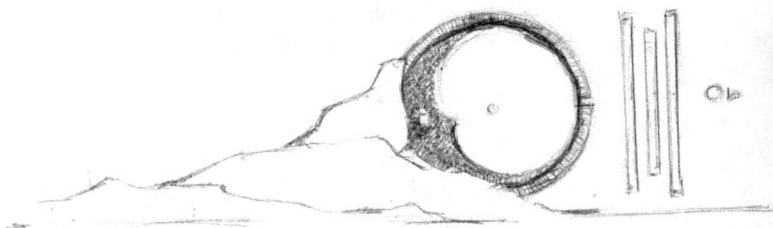

David Burton

CHAPTER TEN

I am in a new building; the surfaces are smooth and reflective. There is a man who is training me to remember what I have forgotten. We saddle the horses – I am communicating with the white one. I walk across the field onto a highway where I find a vehicle with a sail. An amazingly beautiful girl is standing beside the sail, searching for knowledge of how to use it. I teach her how to release the sails, and she flies away.

I return to the building and receive white clothes; I have chosen this, or it has chosen me.

There is a disagreement between two different tribes of people. A way to resolve the conflict is presented and a challenge issued – the son returned with blazing eyes, accepting the challenge, and the younger brother stepping forward to take up the fight. The people who win will gain protection from radiation and something else contained within it, or related to it.

The prince warrior, confident, assured – standing in faith has come. He is awe inspiring. I see the girl who sails standing near a doorway and I follow her into the room. She is so beautiful that the words I have are inadequate to describe her. We talk about her sailing and I am so very impressed with her. I feel alive in her presence; my spirit lifts; my mind connects. We are supposed to be together, in communication, relation, presence, being – love. She is in my arms as I run my hands over her face, looking into her eyes. I touch her hair and trace the curves of her body. We speak a different language.

"I didn't expect this to happen," she says.

"Neither did I," I reply.

"I love you," she says in another language. I hear *tumar vi*. I look into her eyes, unleashing my emotion, expressing my love with all I can: body, mind, soul.

"Please teach me," I ask her, revealing the inside of my being. Our moment together soon comes to an end, as she must leave. I watch until she is out of sight.

When she is gone I walk out the back door of the building and decide to cross the field to see the horses. The white horse is waiting for me and playfully comes to me; we go to see the others.

❦ 3 ❦

I am walking through the tall grass beside the water; rain falls continuously from the sky. I am nearly naked. I walk home. When I arrive, I change my clothes and prepare to leave again. I have very long hair, with a scarf tied around my mouth, and a toque on my head.

"My recovery is mine and mine alone. This is my boundary."

FLASH. I witness the new spacecraft for the human race being created. A triangular shaped craft [*shuttle*] is in the center. Three jets lock on to each corner of the craft; this gives it the lift required to exit the atmosphere. It is called –

❦ 4 ❦

I am standing in front of a building with a blonde haired girl. She is a robot, wearing skin. The house belongs to the man who designed cybernetics, which are now common place in the world; however, someone is trying to kill him and they are using his creation to do it. The girl is the only one immune to this virus. She defends him several times, destroying the attackers. He decides to fake his own death and takes the shape of another being, hiding within their ranks undetected.

There is a series of robotic people designed to be sex slaves. Some humans find in these what they can't find in the world: pleasure and release.

❦ 5 ❧

I am in a room with several other people; they are attempting to summon demons. A man in a black coat appears within the square of their focus. He realizes what is happening; I chase him and take his cloak from him.

❦ 6 ❧

I am walking into a kitchen for the first time; I walk around the equipment and see many things that are wrong. The manager of the restaurant tries to turn me into a slave, but I reject this idea. I have confidence within myself.

FLASH. I am fighting with a man inside a colorful, cube shaped room; music is playing loudly, echoing off the walls and resonating inside me. I throw the man through the wall; he is very angry.

FLASH. I am at a pay phone calling someone for crack cocaine. I tell him I will be there soon, and ask if he has found my credit card. He says, *yes*. I hang up, get in the truck and drive to the hotel. I arrive at the hotel and ascend the stairs, carrying a lamp. When I arrive at the door I am asked to leave the light outside of the room. I am in such a hurry to get high that I place the lamp on the floor beside the door, and walk quickly inside.

A girl is kneeling beside a small glass table; a man [*maybe a pastor; doesn't appear right*] leaves after a few words. As soon as he leaves the drugs come out of the pocket. The man and the girl load, fire and inhale. I desire what my eyes see; yet, I awake before I do something stupid.

❦ 7 ❧

I have found my wings and fly, lifting from the ground and moving through the air. I feel complete. I land, talk to someone, run to the edge and jump. My wings catch the air and I glide to the water below: a stream.

A girl is there, sitting at the water's edge, leaning against a tree. Behind the tree is a room, and within the room is an evil creature who wears the skin of a man. He stands on an ice seal with someone trapped beneath the ice.

I experience an overwhelming urge to free the one below; my first attempt is using a knife to break through the surface. I pierce the frozen element and blood begins pouring up out of the ice, spilling over the floor. I fear that I have now started killing the one I am here to save. I try to give the man money: a payment in exchange for freedom of the one beneath the ice. He refuses. The situation is becoming desperate; more blood is being lost.

"Don't look," I say to the girl. "You don't want to see this." I enter the room and fight the evil. He shatters into black slime and insect like creatures, but he is soon trying to reassemble himself. I destroy the remnants with fire and the room changes. There is a bag full of ecstasy where he used to stand, laying on the floor.

FLASH. A woman leads me up a snow covered mountain to a house; the house is warm, spacious and well lit with light. I don't understand why we are here. She has tricked me somehow – we are trapped here temporarily. She is evil and tries to hurt me with emotions: betrayal, anger, rejection.

❧ **8** ☙

I go on a journey, one that takes me to a distant city. I take one man and one woman with me; their strength is weakness. As we approach the city they are distracted by an old wrecked concrete building. We enter. It is soon apparent that the place is evil and there are several people sitting on concrete benches, smoking crack cocaine – their eyes are dead, lost, and empty. The girl I am with sits down and the man starts talking to them.

One person on the bench offers the smoke to me and I freak out. I want nothing to do with this. I leave, taking the people I came with: the girl is already lost; she can't hear me. Her eyes are changing. The man falls; I reach down and pick him up. We finally exit the building.

FLASH. I am in a classroom; someone switches my book for one that looks similar, but has no text in it. I am angry and begin searching for my book. I find two copies that are similar, but I get angrier with each copy. In the end, I discover it is a girl who has taken my book. I wake up screaming,

"WHERE IS IT!?"

~ **9** ~

I am near the ocean, searching for a place to stay. It does not take long to find a place; however, the building is strangely designed: the basement leads to caverns that open onto beach coves. One of these rooms has a glass wall that separates me from the sand. A beautiful blonde girl is coming to see me; we are linked in some way: similar. She arrives and we unite; we are supposed to be together but something interferes.

FLASH. I am in the same building, but in a different section. There are several people gathered here around a table and I feel insignificant. The table is in a small courtyard. Someone has designed this theatre to play on my insecurity and doubts, impacting me emotionally. The girl at my side abandons me and my emotional reaction peaks.

I stand, leave the table, and walk to the center of the concrete clearing. I jump into the air and float gently back to earth. I see a building and a tall fence, keeping us from freedom. I begin climbing the building, the people at the table start freaking out, and I awake.

~ **10** ~

I am on the top of a mountain; there are many animals here. I seem to be able to communicate with them. I watch the birds fly over the water, as a lion sniffs at my hand. I walk further up the path and come to a grassy hill, which overlooks the ocean. Two mice play in the blades of grass. There is a girl planting seed or tending to a garden. I remember speaking with her briefly as I passed her on the way up here.

FLASH. I am standing outside a house, watching events unfold. I am many people at once, and watch several events simultaneously.

I am returning from another world and get into an argument with my parent because he does not know where I've been. He has to go to work, but does not want to leave me unattended because I travelled without permission.

I am the older brother now. I stand up and say that I will look after him. I tell my parent that no one else will look after this.

FLASH. The male parent is working in an old house with another scientist; they sit at a table, assembling all the small pieces that have been laid out. A woman enters the room. I believe they had plans together, but the man rejects the plans, and her.
She leaves with quiet dignity, seemingly unaffected by this whole exchange, as if she is used to it. I watch as she walks out the door into another room. She speaks, but I can't hear her. She walks out the door at the far end of the room and I hear a crash. I run to the doorway and descend a flight of steps: she lay at the base, broken and bleeding.

FLASH. I am in a dimly lit room of some kind. I am with a man and woman; the man is evil and the woman is his slave. I have cocaine in my pocket: one hard, one soft. Someone is giving a class; they say, make a pipe and inhale. I make the pipe and inhale once while it is empty.

Something happens. I am shielded from the action that would have eventually come next. Instead I walk into the washroom and flush the contents of my pocket; it crumbles in my fingertips as I toss it into the water.
FLASH. I stand over the body of the woman; she has turned blue and I fear that she has died. I take her in my arms; to my surprise she wraps her arms around me. She is alive. I run up the stairs, screaming to get help – my voice is gone, something is preventing me from calling out.

David Burton

❧ 11 ❧

I am in a school. I have barricaded myself inside of it – a woman comes to see me. We discuss something I have forgotten.

FLASH. I am in a meeting, sitting behind two girls; I take a lock of her hair. I am going to clone her. As I walk away, I look back and see the younger of the two checking me out. I am surprised and pleased.

❧ 12 ❧

I am talking to a young teenage girl on a gravel road in the early evening; night has begun to fall. I am speaking to her about alcoholism and drug addiction; although I don't directly reference it, or use these two words. My voice is old and raspy, I am much older than I am now. I talk about drinking one bottle, then two – and not getting drunk.

I tell her that a time will come when it will no longer work for her. She says, *not if I am using other drugs*. I tell her that even those too will stop working. She can sense the honesty; the truth in my voice, and words. She has, for there is, no defense against the truth.

FLASH. I am in church; a service is taking place. I am struggling with finding a way to tell them that their world will end in fire. My hand gets caught in something – a woman comes to free it. I know things about the people and the world, and it is quickly apparent to those around me that I could have no possible way of knowing what I know. Soon, the people begin to call me by the name: prophet.

❧ 13 ❧

I am standing in nothingness; there are these creatures here that look human but are not. I walk around the circle and look into the dead eyes of each, trying to communicate.

FLASH. I am on the Island, walking down a concrete path. An addict that is trying to help me (in his mind) is following, trying to force his will upon me and my life. I run to the edge, call the wind and lift up off the ground. I glide and land. There are now two people [*demons*] attempting to cut off the path. They have not seen my first flight. I have little choice. I lift off the ground, circle around and land on the shoulders of the second, slamming his head into the ground.

The fight is joined and now both are trying to kill me; their *help* is going to see me dead. One comes for me and I attack, taking his head in my hands, and breaking his skull repeatedly against the bark of a nearby tree. I had attempted to fly and leave the battle before it escalated, but they dragged me down to earth and into war.

The other removes a weapon and fires. Several bullets pierce my skin, entering my body. Three more enter my head. I feel each slicing through the skin and the pressure of compression. The battle ends when I look up and say,

"You've shot me three times in the head; is it enough?"

They flee, terrified.

⤳ 14 ⤶

I am in a small dimly lit house; there are two sets of tiger striped kittens, each with distinct markings. They are playfully fighting amongst themselves, yet it is obvious that it could quickly turn into a claws extended true fight.

FLASH. A large cat (much larger than a man) stands outside the window in the yard, peering through the glass. It has several sets of ears: extensions from its body. I can see the evil it contains; it quickly turns and finds my presence. It races toward me and slams crashing into the glass: the glass holds true. I feel the impact concussion wave as I awake.

⤳ 15 ⤶

I am in a distant land, walking beside the ocean near a tree line, heading toward an unknown destination. There are several young native women here; I talk to one of them: her eyes are beautiful.

David Burton

FLASH. I am sitting at a fire that blazes light in the darkness of night; people have gathered here to watch others stand near the fire and speak. I sit next to a beautiful woman; she turns and speaks to me: telling me of a prophecy of myself.

"You must go back into the woods to find what you are looking for," she says quietly.

"What will happen if I go?" I ask.

"You will die [*be returned*]," she replies.

"I do not fear death, but I don't want to go back out there. Look at me, what if they reject me?"

FLASH. I am walking back to my cabin in the woods; I look to make sure no one is around then I lift from the ground and glide the entire way. I enter the cabin and discovered it is adjoined with another woman. I ask her about the prophetic words; she tells me of a spiritual system. I communicate with a scholar, far away: a letter arrives. It contains strange symbols and a silver dragon. I tell the woman that I am deciding to stay and search; or, leave.

❦ 16 ❧

I stand before a screen; my hand is raised: I am to control the object [*a circle; sphere*] with my mind and gesture.

FLASH. My knowledge and power are to be tested in the ring. I face several people and practice the gift. I am inexperienced and push too hard: the objects go flying.

❦ 17 ❧

I am standing in a green field; I haven't been here for a very long time, but I remember throwing the ball around with my father as a child in this same field. A girl stands beside me; a girl I have been searching for. I recognize her for who she truly is and we speak about the dream world. I can't remember specifically. I ask her to stay with me within the dream, but she refuses, saying,

"Our characters grow weak here." I am angry at her rejection and become frustrated. What is the use of this world if she will not be with me?

"I will destroy this world then." I throw my hands upward and release power – the first attempt has little result. I do it again. I feel the release and cracks form around me. I know I am close to shattering the world. I push hard and sections of reality start falling away in pieces, revealing raw raging power in color, behind the illusionary walls of reality.

FLASH. I attempt to seize the power.

FLASH. I awake in the bottom deck of a ship with other people around me; I am dirty, covered in human filth. I stumble into another room and see people from my dream setting up for a meeting. I attempt to talk to them, but none know what I am saying. They begin to look at me with condemnation in their eyes. I leave the room and find that I am in a hospital.

I am cleaning up the dishes from the meeting when I realize a family member is having surgery. The doctor makes the injury worse. I go to the fountain to splash water on my face. While standing there, another family member recognizes me, and asks when I got back. We go for coffee. I start asking about how long I've been gone, but they misunderstand and ask,

"Are you taking medication?"

My anger surges and I can feel my eyes blazing. I feel the power rising up with me, and I want nothing more than to give in to the temptation.

"Fuck medication."

Soon I awake again, this time here.

❧ 18 ❧

I am racing toward a closed gateway; I speak a word which sparks something within me. The gateway opens and I pass through, spiraling through the air, kick flip spiral. I draw on the source of power and feel the current raging within me, gathering. I extend my arm and hear a choir of angels singing a chorus: so beautiful – the sound, the source, the spin.

I release the power surging through me and watch it appear in the air before me, and explode against the target below. It pulsess from my fingertips as a blue fireball, interwoven with lightning.

I rise, wings extended, and draw upon the source again, once more feeling it gather within me. I extend both arms, palms together and unleash fury.

[*Draw, hold: release.*]

I hear a voice, echoing inside my mind.

"There are two demons standing beside the door."

FLASH. I am standing in a room with a single bed; there is a girl in the bed. I open a gateway [*portal*] for looking into the other world. She peers through, but can't find them. Time is of the essence, so I slip through the gateway, drawing on the source in the same moment.

I stand in the same room, yet another dimensional world. I am filled with power, but still can't see those I hunt visually. So I unleash red, orange, yellow interwoven flames in a concussion circle: extending outward in waves. I am standing in the center. The power of the flames casts a shadow, exposing where they are.

❧ 19 ❧

I am in a school, making contact and avoiding something; eventually, the others find me and we go outside. We fly to the roof and two of us confront the other. We each have a pail of white paint that is connected to us, but his is empty. We know that it is because he has lost his faith in God.

"You are an angel; you must talk to God."

He attempts it. The bucket fills with a brown liquid; we are concerned at what this means because it appears black to us at first. He says something else. I put my hands in the liquid.
"It is brown," I exclaim. He speaks again. I place my hands deep inside the liquid and stir. It becomes white; the black comes out quickly – it was only a thin layer at the top, like oil.

FLASH. I am standing on the sand near the ocean; the tide is far out into the bay and I walk along the water's edge. Two women are with me, women from my past. I walk with one of them along the ocean water. My hair is long and falls to each side of my face; I tuck it behind my ears. We walk arm in arm. I feel complete acceptance from her, the pain of years gone by has been washed away. When we get closer, the other woman comes to me and wraps her arms around me. I feel my spirit soar into the sky. I feel her hands around me, holding tightly; I feel her against me. I run my fingers through her hair.

"I've been dreaming of this for years." I feel amazing, and complete.

๏ **20** ๏

I am standing in the darkness; a creature made of bone and muscle tissue in the shape of a wolf attacks me. I feel its teeth sink into the flesh of my calf. I draw my sword and sever it limb from limb, finishing by splitting its rib cage in half. I ascend the stairs quickly to find a girl bound by a demon shade, clinging to her back with its arms wrapped around her neck and feet around her thighs.

I touch her, offering my shield to encompass her – the demon slides off and disappears [*dispels*]. I descend once more and am confronted by a fire demon; he burns brightly – red, orange, blue, white in the darkness. We stand: facing each other, waiting.

David Burton

FLASH. I stand upon a tower, far above the earth; a city lay beneath. A cord extends from the building, descending to the earth. I hold on to this line with bare hands and slide down. I watch the buildings grow closer during the descent. I am concerned about friction causing my hands to burst into flame; yet, they remain strong and cold.

I doubt for nothing.

David Burton

My tongue is the pen of a
ready writer.

Psalm 45:1

ἄγγελος

MESSENGER

David Burton

CHAPTER ELEVEN

I am in a large banquet hall. Many people are here. A girl walks into the party with crack cocaine in her hand. She talks quietly to her friend, looking for a pipe. Everyone sits in stunned silence; no one wants to talk to her. I stand up and walk toward her. They are shocked that she has been given entrance to the banquet. In their eyes, she is not worthy to be among them.

"Why do you all condemn her?" I ask.

In frustration, I take her hand and lead her outside. I spread my wings and launch myself into the air. It has been a long time since I've flown, and I am surprised more than anything else. People mock me as I fly, but nothing can bring me down.

FLASH. I am standing in a large hall, playing guitar with someone I don't recognize. Several strings snap because I am playing in a fury. Darkness descends as we walk outside. I see several people wandering in the night, lost and using drugs. My acquaintance leaves, but I sit down, and continue playing.

"Open the eyes of my heart, Lord. Open the eyes of my heart – I want to see you." I sing into the black of night. As I play, I begin to hear evil rushing toward me, exiting the darkness.

❦ 2 ❧

I have not yet resisted unto blood, striving against sin, yet if that is what you require of me then so be it.

❦ 3 ❧

The first thing I remember is a beautiful woman trying to bind me, by placing a ring on my finger. I take it off with my teeth, and spit it into the water. She has lost the battle.

FLASH. I am standing in a room with my parents. They ask me to stay, but I refuse. It hurts me that I am disobeying my parent's wishes for me. I want to please them, but I can't.

"Do you want me to die slowly, or live?"

I am half conscious, half asleep, stuck in the dream while this is happening. I am speaking out loud inside my room.

༺ **4** ༻

I am brought before the courts of law where a man is falsely accusing me of something. I may have to go to jail and I am angry. I take this man aside into another room and face him. I start praying in another language and talking to the demons inside the man. I cast them out of his body in the name of Jesus Christ. It is a battle because they do not want to leave.

I wake up from this dream and find the man surrounded by people. He is talking about his dream and how I freed him from the demons that plagued his life. He says never to doubt.

Then I wake up; this time for real.

༺ **5** ༻

I arrive on the site of an abandoned hotel. It is crumbling from age, and is now blazing with a fire in its lower levels. I am a fireman. I start laying out hose and attaching it to the hydrant, getting ready to fight the fire. No one else is around. I turn on the water and wrestle the hose to the ground. I aim the hose above the flames and rain water down upon it.

Other people start arriving just as the first fire starts going out, but I know it has spread to other parts of the old building – hidden and waiting to be unleashed. The iron in the front of the structure is collapsing; the fire captain approaches to inspect. I see a piece of steel falling straight toward him and I run to save his life. I tackle him to the ground, removing him from harm's way, and he narrowly escapes death.

David Burton

We enter the building to search for survivors. It appears that homeless people live here, and most likely started the fire. We find a man who is drinking alcohol, and mourning the loss of his girl. He says she is dead. We tell him to leave, and continue searching.

We find a room filled with women's clothes. A wall has collapsed and the sun is shining through the opening. The sky is filled with the spectrum colors of dawn. She walks into the room and I am surprised. I tell her that everyone thinks she is dead, and now is the time to leave this place and seek a new life.

I awaken in the early morning.

❧ 6 ☙

I awake, not knowing where I am, or who I am.

FLASH. I travel to the ocean and dive off a cliff into the sea.

FLASH. I am given a gift, a book about becoming a disciple.

❧ 7 ☙

I meet a girl, my high school girlfriend. We get together, working and living together. Then I meet another girl and I want to leave my girlfriend, but the new girl is offended because I haven't left her yet.

The new girl seems so far away [*unattainable*] that I give up and sleep with my old girlfriend. I awake just as she removes her clothes.

❧ 8 ☙

I am with the girl I love, and I want to become closer to her, to know her more. The world interferes and tears us apart. I wake up and pray. I am filled with love, and peace is upon me.

❦ 9 ❧

A using dream. I am completely horrified. I hate myself right now. After everything that has happened I cooked crack and smoked it. I awake feeling hopeless and disappointed.

❦ 10 ❧

I speak with a man about my journal. He has found my artwork and is wondering how it is possible. Meanwhile, I have discovered women living in this place and have bonded with one in particular. I go to her and we hold each other, our hands lock together and we walk through the dream until I awake.

❦ 11 ❧

I am with several others and we are raiding another clan's house; we are inside, rolling up their sleeping blankets when they arrive. We exit the building and face them outside. Several of our group attempt to lie, but the truth is discovered. Many flee.

I run to the cliff side near me and see a river raging below. I do not hesitate – I step off the edge into the air and descend to the riverbank in flight. I land and think I have escaped; however, they send warriors after me through a different path.

They attack with weapons; I turn their own weapons against them and take them prisoner. I return with them to the house and force peace to be made. While I was gone I find that other creatures have arrived, called *the who*.

FLASH. I am on a plane flying in the darkness of night; I see the stars shining brightly outside the window. Suddenly the plane drops and I am outside, seeing the plane from a different perspective as an engine dies and falls. The engine starts again and the aircraft levels out.

Then I am within again, standing near the captain. He is discussing landing the plane. I get the impression it is hostile ground because he mentions the forest and how we will not survive the night.

David Burton

The plane shakes and again I am outside, watching the plane descend and land in the meadow between the trees.

I awake; and, sleep once more.

I am standing near the ocean studying something. An aircraft approaches and hovers close by. It has a flat bottom and fans that guide its direction are mounted on the top. It spins in a manner that should not be possible without something holding it up in the air.

I have seen this craft before in a restricted access military base, and last time it carried equipment. This time it is filled with seats and people are watching. It is enclosed with a glass canopy, which is not immediately visible until it lands in the water, submerging partially for a moment. Water rolls off the canopy and the craft floats on the water.

FLASH. I am studying a touch screen on which there are icons for control, molecular genetic level and language. Off to one side is a weapons panel. I am standing with another person and show him how the panel has awakened.

When any of the icons are slid, they snap back into place. The weapons are glowing with light inside their icon; this is new. I have known this panel for awhile and after the war, the light faded from the weapons, rendering them useless, but something has happened and the weapons are now active again. I explain this and awake.

⁓ 12 ⤳

I am on a beach, and waves are crashing against the shore. A tent is nearby and three women are in it; I want to have sex with all of them, but a storm is coming.

A man appears and walks out to the water's edge to meet the storm. War ships are everywhere, scattered upon the sea. The man sails into the storm and is lost.

FLASH. There is a man who is a gifted speaker, a preacher, and when he talks people accept whatever he is saying. He can sell anything to anyone.

FLASH. I go to see my parents to ask them how I was conceived. While I am there my enemy sends two assassins to take my life. Instead, I tell them the truth about their master, and defeat them.

⚜ 13 ⚜

I just killed a man.

A man approaches me, intent on violence. He wants to engage me in battle, but I continuously refuse and walk away several times. He pursues me, still trying to provoke me. I hold my ground, until he threatens my family.

Something inside of me snaps, and I hit him. He stumbles, and I hit him again. This time he falls to the ground, but I do not stop. I keep pounding until he lay unmoving on the ground. I run away, searching for a place to hide because I know the authorities will come to arrest me.

I find an old building that is easy to gain access to and enter. There are a few old offices here, a perfect place to hide in. I want to know if my sister is alright. She disappeared the moment the man attacked me, and I never had the chance to find her afterward.

FLASH. I get in an argument with someone who is trying to help me. I tell him there are certain things I can't do. I almost get in a fight with him, and his *shining eyes* before I wake.

⚜ 14 ⚜

Before I close my eyes, I ask God for my wings. He says,

FLASH. I reach one hand to my right and catch the air; I reach one hand to my left and catch the air. Once the air is in the palm of my hand, I am lifted from the ground. I do it twice consecutively. I am slowly being restored.

FLASH. I have become involved with a woman and we have a daughter. I have been gone from their life for some time, but now have returned. I go in to see my daughter's room and talk. When I tell her about Jesus, she asks why her mother doesn't know him. I can't believe she can walk and talk already.

FLASH. I take a friend to go solve an injustice. The office is high up in an tower. We walk into a closed meeting and confront the people.

"I have worked with this client for a long time and at the last moment you steal them from me?" I am angry. I tell the client to get a new company because this one is dishonest. As we are leaving, someone comments, saying,

"They only care about money and living forever."

"Jesus is the only way to eternal life," I say as we walk out of the room and enter the elevator. A man follows us to wreak havoc. I see him for what he is, his eyes give him away. I begin to pray. He is in the corner, withdrawing and curling into a ball. He tries to come at us.

"I bind you, Satan." I yell. The man is thrown across the elevator and into the corner. He comes again.

"I bind you, Satan!" I scream. Again he is thrown back as the doors open behind us. My friend loses it and runs away screaming. The man approaches one last time.

"Satan, ask God forgiveness and see what happens." I have a strange sense of compassion. The doors close as I step outside.

Moments later the building starts emptying of people, all hell has broken loose. Paramedics arrive and a couple of people are taken out on stretchers. A crowd has formed and I figure out that another member of my team has been left behind somehow.

I turn to the people and say, "Every man, woman and child who is a Christian – I need your help right now. I need you to pray for [*name*]."

I am standing in confidence, unashamed of my belief, unshaken by battle, complete in Christ and resting in his power. My voice speaks clearly and with depth; the call has gone out.

15

Dreams that slip through my fingers like dry sand.

16

I am praying and helping other people; one day I am going downtown and I pick up. I search everywhere to find more, but can't. Then I find a leader and tell him about this experience: it all seems like a dream.

FLASH. I am in a crowd of people and I get called up to preach. I am wearing a suit. I stand up and speak about grace, blood, repentance, and the power that comes with it. I open my mouth and the words are placed inside it.

"I haven't gone this long without a cigarette since I was twelve years old." People start walking away. I stop, saying,

"There is more, but not for you now."

17

I experienced some strange conscious communication: in the body, yet out of it at the same time and denied the memory of the words spoken. It is powerful.

FLASH. I awake inside a refuge filled with people. I ascend the steps, seeking the person who operates it. I ascend the stairway inside

David Burton

the refuge and pass a girl on the stairs; I am drawn to her. She reaches out and wraps her arms around me.

"I love you," she whispers. She lets go and walks down the stairs. I approach the director.

"What is her ability?" I ask. I need to know because I think she is about to leave.

"She broadcasts emotions," is the reply. I run after her and take her into my arms. I run my fingers over her skin and she responds. Suddenly I become aware of the people in the dining hall, everyone has stopped and is staring at me.

Then all hell breaks loose; warriors are coming. People scatter. I stand to defend the girl, but there are so many.

FLASH. Having sex with an evil girl.

FLASH. I am in the city, and people pass by me as I walk the streets. I pulse light and it reduces the people to ash. I brush it off my skin, saying,

> "This is war, you understand."

I search for her, I know she is being held in a building inside the city. I am drawn toward her, and I am using a device that alters time. I enter the building and free the captives. The soldiers that hold them stand at a distance. They know I will kill all of them if they do not obey me.

18

I am in a foreign country, helping people. I am travelling from my house to a village. It is such a long journey that coming home at night, I walk in darkness – so I take these berries that glow in the dark and line my path with them.

19

I am in a world completely destroyed by war, buildings are crumbling, and people wander the streets, lost and hopeless. Famine has taken the land. The western world was completely dependent upon grocery stores and restaurants for their food; now society has fallen apart and they have lost the skill of providing for themselves. A group of us travel through this world searching for others and trying to restore some sense of reason and sanity. It is snowing.

FLASH. I come across a group of soldiers inside a house; they have lost their desire to fight and have become enslaved. Someone with me confronts their master, and takes away his power. I offer the soldiers a chance to fight for something again. They respond and follow us out into the destroyed city.

❦ 20 ❦

I stand by the ocean,
And the waters inside;
For the dreams that are coming:
From the power inside.

I am playing guitar in a high tower that overlooks the ocean. I keep everyone out; this is my sanctuary. I warm up with a few chords then I feel *called*. I descend from the tower and walk out onto the sand. I am standing on the beach and the waves come crashing toward me.

I start playing and writing music. I write two verses, which I have forgotten. I am playing and singing. Suddenly the chorus enters my mind and I play it; the ocean responds and becomes raging. I am playing inside a storm. I feel the presence of God, I know his power, and I am truly alive.

I awake from this dream inside of another dream where I am telling someone about this experience: "You can't take my guitar away because it is here," I point to my mind.

I awake and return to sleep.

I sleep only to continue my education in faith and flight. I am pursued by my enemies. I climb the side of a building and launch myself from its rooftop into the air. They try to follow, but I turn in flight and strike them to the ground.

David Burton

"I am angel," I yell back at them in a strange language. I return to a building where I used to reside, but I am transformed – I have risen.

I see things happen before they occur, I know things other people have no way of knowing. I fight against the demonic forces hidden among the people. It is not on my own that I do these things: it is the power of God within me.

> *I stand by the ocean,*
> *Where the waters reside;*
> *For the dreams that are coming*
> *From the waters inside.*

I awake from the night with something new within me; I feel it: it is residing. I have experienced the substance of my hope and heard evidence of the unseen.

21

I am visiting my children when I learn that a man has moved in with the mother of my children, and has enslaved them. I talk to my daughter, asking about this situation. She says they work all the time, can't play with friends, and their every action is controlled.

I am furious. When he returns in his car I run toward him, take a baseball bat and beat him to death. I free my children.

David Burton

Every one that is of the truth
heareth my voice.

John 18:37

David Burton

CHAPTER TWELVE

I am travelling the night again, trying to save a girl who I once loved; however, she doesn't want to talk to me and sends a group of people to stop me. I annihilate them physically and then come to her, pick her up and carry her out.

"I am not the boy you once knew," I say.

❦ 2 ❧

I am kayaking. When we stop for rest near the shore of the river, someone comes at me with a knife. I grab him and throw him against the wall.

"I could kill you," I say. Then I pray for him. When I let him go, he runs away. We return to the kayak and into the water.

❦ 3 ❧

What a nightmare, crack cocaine everywhere. I am buying it, people are smoking it. A girl in the room becomes infected with an alien virus; a creature gestates within her and then falls from her host body, but the demon can't survive because of the atmosphere.

❦ 4 ❧

I am inside a building, standing within an old abandoned library. I find the girl I love among a few people who are hiding from the world. I come and offer myself to her, making my presence known as we talk together.

The demons come quickly, trying to separate us. I protect her, suppressing attack after attack. Another girl tries to get my attention and seduce me, offering herself to me. I make the choice to stay with the girl I love.

FLASH. I am working in a kitchen; I am running the place and in charge of the restaurant next door. I find the cooks next door doing

Wall Between Worlds

a few things wrong and I become very upset. They cook the food long before the order comes in so that it goes bad. I tell them the whole point of the restaurant is to serve freshly prepared dishes.

I wake up, and somewhere in the night there is an earthquake. My entire bed is shaking for several moments. I don't understand what is happening. Then it is gone.

FLASH. I am in a house with a girl; I feel the presence of something. I run outside, down a pathway, and emerge into a clearing among the trees. There is a gray sky above me and a wooden board walkway beneath. I see lightning flashing around the base of an invisible circular object.

᷇ 5 ᷈

A preacher comes to town with a big tent and several large television screens; he is having a conference and many people are invited. He puts on a good show, but it truly is evil beneath; he comes only for the money. He talks about good things but runs a pornography business on the side. I tell him he is going to lose everything unless he stops; other people in town want to kill him

᷇ 6 ᷈

I am in a recovery program away from society but the people who run it arrange something unknown to me. The police come and arrest me, taking me to jail. I bring my cow with me. He is huge, standing taller than me.

The police don't tell me I am under arrest, and don't charge me, they just throw me in jail. Soon, I am sent into town for a blood test. I flee as soon as I can. I go to a family residence and tell them what has happened. They ask about my cow. I don't know what to tell them.

I feel frustrated as I open the front door and walk out onto the porch. Blue sky stretches as far as the eye can see, over a crystal blue green ocean. Several large rocks like a cliff face stand on either side of me. I am elevated, looking out from the top of the cliff. The waves crash at the base and the sun shines brightly in the sky. I am awestruck by its beauty. I use a camera to take several pictures: left, right and center – to capture the panorama of the view.

Someone dies in our house, and I start taking apart the body, trying to repair the damage. While I am standing over him he begins to move. I have resurrected him by mistake. I freak out, unsure if he will experience pain from the damage of his body. I try to hold him down and send his soul back to the grave, but he is resilient and overpowers me.

He is standing, unsure of what has happened; I explain it to him. He is surprisingly alright with it and approaches life with a new fervor. I tell him about my problem and he accompanies me to the prison where the authorities know him. The situation is resolved, and I am set free.

FLASH. I am standing on the Island, listening to three female creatures with wings, buried in the sand. The center one leads the speech and talks about various gods, trying to confuse people as to who God is. I am angry and approach them. I stand in front of them and speak the name of the LORD.

I can't remember what I say, but part of it is a scathing rebuke and each word I speak causes them to retreat further into the sand, as though they can't stand to be in the presence of the truth.

Near the end I feel a sharp sting in my hand, something trying to embed itself in my skin. I end my words and leave them. I did not come to cause a war, just give confession.

FLASH. I come to in the middle of a hockey game being played on broken ice, a lake ice frozen during a winter storm. I am playing goaltender, but I not only defend my net, but attack the other.

FLASH. I am standing in the inner city, walking away from something I have forgotten. I lose my sense of direction and pass through a women's dormitory much like our own, except there are only four to a room. I stop and trade one piece of jewelry for another; the woman smiles, she is pleased with the trade.

Wall Between Worlds

They do not think it is strange that I am passing through their house as I continue on my journey. I exit the building and see the housing complex is near a lake, with an entranceway that is marked with pillars and arches.

I continue into the poverty stricken core of the inner city and end up standing at a chain link fence. People have gathered here and are going in and out of a ground level building. I think it is a homeless shelter, but someone tells me it is a youth hostel.

I walk around the fence and try to engage several people in conversation, but they are afraid of me. I reach out to them, trying to carry the message of God, but none will hear me.

I awake, but, to the people around me in this world,
my day hasn't even started yet.

❧ 7 ❧

I am in a classroom, playing guitar until it is taken away. A man is standing in an open doorway, teaching the class. We travel through the doorway and are sitting next to a fire that has gone out. The man is talking, as I fall asleep.

I awaken in the darkness.

"Is anyone awake?" I cry. "We have to pray."

And then it comes and takes hold of me, dragging me through the night and emerging high above the earth, in the black sky.

It happens in the blink of an eye, and I start screaming the words I know will save me, trying to wake from this world. I fight with all the strength I have within me, knowing I will be trapped and helpless if I do not.

I awake screaming the words into the night: "In the name of our Lord and Saviour Jesus Christ, I cast out all evil!"

I lay in the darkness of night upon my bed and consider; my enemy is practiced in deception. So I return to sleep and walk straight into the next dream.

This time it is a girl from my past who gives me a ring. I get the impression that she is returning the ring I gave her, although I can't remember giving her one. I find out she is married.

We are alone together in a room; at first she is just a picture on the screen: naked and under water. I respond sexually. She emerges from the screen and becomes flesh. She dances naked around the room and I react, taking off my clothes. She is whispering inside my inside my head as we dance.

"It's okay," she says, "We are allowed to do this. You can do anything you want to, just don't touch me." I can't resist, I get on my knees, grab hold of her and stretch out my tongue.

I wake up consumed with lust. I can't think and my mind burns with the vision. I walk to the washroom and finish what she started.

Then, in a moment of clarity, I see the night in its entirety and fall on my knees in prayer, asking forgiveness. It becomes obvious that my enemy knows my weakness, and my weakness becomes glaringly obvious to me, as though a curtain has been pulled back.

He couldn't get me in one way, so he came in another.
Once more I return to sleep and slip quickly into the next dream. This one is already fading with the morning light so I will keep it brief and to the point.

I am standing in the sand on a beach, facing the point with the ocean behind me. I see a hole that someone has dug next to the base of a cliff, and tried to bury something. I am curious so I kneel down and search through the objects.

I find photographs, envelopes, a sweater and a meth pipe. What I am looking at is the story of someone's life, a night of partying on the beach that did not end well.

She appears out of nowhere, maybe a cloud. She is a teenage girl who looks innocent, but she is sad as though she has been crying. She sits with me in the sand and we talk about her life. I offer her a way out. I will take her home with me, away from this life of misery.

~❧ **8** ☙~

I am living in a house with a gorgeous woman that I have fallen in love with. I sleep close to her just because I want to be next to her, but there is evil in the house. She falls under a spell, and taking a knife, she tries to cut herself. I knock the blade out of her hand before she has a chance to draw blood, rescuing her. The dark spell spreads like an infection through the house, turning everything it touches to evil – until we send it back where it came from.

~❧ **9** ☙~

I am walking with a preacher, or someone; we are talking about being healed.

~❧ **10** ☙~

I feel the call to sleep; I obey the call. I fall into bed, pull the covers around me. And WHAM I am in the spirit:

I awaken to the darkness.

"Is anyone awake?" I cry out. This cry is becoming familiar. "We have to pray." I say these words again and I become aware completely of the presence all around me. I am not alone. My voice and hearing are crystal clear, but I can see nothing with my eyes except the waves of a black velvet cloth.

"I am just a man," I begin to say, and with each word I begin to shrivel away from the presence. I can feel myself collapsing. And then I claim something within me and I snap:

"I am a man," I scream the first part of the sentence. I am standing true, in power and faith. I do not have the words to explain the transformation occurring inside of me in a single flash of light. Waking and completing the sentence simultaneously,

"And I will walk in the image of my father."

❦ 11 ❦

I am in a house. I have a high powered computer system that I watch pornography on. I am living with two girls. I am naked, wrapped in a blanket, with a pair of panties in my hand when they both emerge from a room naked and invite me into the hot tub.

FLASH. I am standing near the house with my dad when a man comes to tell me that the house is sold and I have to move. I freak out, screaming at the man that he told us we could stay for a long time. I throw him out while my dad tries to restrain me.

FLASH. More naked woman; this one on a screen (yet flesh at the same time), playing with her breasts, legs spread open. I try to hold on to this vision, but it slips away as I partially wake for a moment.

Then I return, and someone tries to kill me while I am hanging out with pornography models.
I time travel and end up at my parents with my sister, and I teach my nephew to say:

"God is good; all the time."

The landscape starts shifting and won't retain itself for more than moments at a time. I become frustrated and wake for the last time.

The first words out of my mouth are:

"Why am I still here? Out of all the places, why did you return me here?"

❦ 12 ❦

I dream of being homeless, broken and destitute; I wake up thoroughly depressed.

Wall Between Worlds

❧ 13 ❧

I am reading a book as the lights come on, and wake me from sleep; the words on the page fade instantly and the memory of them is torn from my mind.

FLASH. I am in a classroom with a box of white salt in front of me; it is below the surface of the desk so I place my hands on it and it begins to increase beneath my palms. I move my fingertips across its rough surface until it is spilling over the side.

I exit the classroom and ascend a staircase to the top of the building. Here several of us are once again training for flight; we step off the building into the air, but we do not fall. Some of us practice with a tether for the first couple of times, but this is a lesson in faith, and we must learn to fly without the harness.

The professor catches us dancing in the air and we explain to him that we have all been rejected by our respective worlds and now we have come here; we do not want to be exposed.

❧ 14 ❧

I am about to read my journal before the people when someone comes to get me and says,

"Bring your journal."

"Why?" I ask.

"We want to discuss your writing, and dreams." They reply. By this time I am in the back office and I completely freak out.

"I don't sleep," I scream. "I can't take it anymore."

I am raging and demons are manifesting in people. A girl in front of me falls on her knees. I stretch my arms out to either side and point with my fingertips; something lifts me from the ground. I return to the ground and have sex with the girl.

David Burton

❧ 15 ❧

I am at a gathering in an auditorium of some kind. I have a conversation with several people and end up hanging out with them when the function ends. I go in search of drugs even though they counsel me against it.

"If they can't accept me as I really am I will reign fire down from the sky and consume them," I say. "If I use once in three months and they still reject me, what good are they to me in my life?"

FLASH. I am sitting at a table. A huge flock of crows fly over us. I tell everyone to take a rock and try to hit one: several of us do, and witches fall from the sky. They sit with us and I ask them what is wrong.

❧ 16 ❧

I am going with someone to see a housing development. While walking through the buildings I meet a girl that I am drawn toward.

"Are you saved?" I ask her. She doesn't know what I am talking about so I tell her about Jesus.

❧ 17 ❧

I fall asleep and within minutes I am attacked by a demon, trapped within the dream.

"This is my room," I say in defense, over and over. I catch a glimpse of its eyes and hear its voice. I start screaming: "Jesus," until I am simply crying his name and awake saying it.

I am wrought with fear; I lay in bed waiting for it to pass. I watch the shadows in my room and prepare to return.

I return to a world where people are lined up in order to receive healing. I feel drunk – my balance is off, my vision is different. I am filled with the spirit. I walk toward the people, ready to unleash this power, and it is now that I realize that I can't hear or speak.

FLASH. I am in a building and one of the people has fallen under some sort of spell, or something: he is catatonic. I go to him, place my hands on his head and say,

"In the name of Jesus Christ, return."

His head snaps up and his eyes open wide. I am pouring power into him as I awake.

I sleep again and return to a classroom; many things are being taught about God, but not the truth. They are words without power — clouds without water. I am very angry and want to destroy the facility; instead I take over teaching the class. I start teaching.

"How many of you know that you have a spirit?" One person nods his head. "That's it? Just one. When I awake in my spirit I cry out for others. This is my cry: I scream, 'Is anyone awake? We have to pray! Satan is coming.'" One person laughs.

"Get out of my class," I say. "Anyone else who doesn't want to be here, leave." One by one, sometimes several at a time, they all exit the building. I am alone and on fire. One woman comes to me and tries to tell me not to teach what I have, and I reply with,

"Awhile ago God came to me and said, will you still love me even if you are the only student that remains?" I take her outside to the ocean where we stand on a cliff that rises above the sea — the sky is growing dark. I tell her to open her bible and read the first words she sees. I open mine and read the first line. (I have forgotten; lost it). I am teaching her to believe; I close my eyes, raise my hands and call power.

"Wind, Lord," I say. I feel it touch my face, moving across my skin. "More, more, more." The storm unleashes it power as the wind rages and lightning begins flashing in the sky. She is afraid, but I tell her to look. Staring at the lightning moving across the clouds, I say,

"His pain is his beauty."

David Burton

ᖗ 18 ᖕ

I am running through the snow, pursuing a young woman, but she is faster than me. We run through the forest on a snow covered path while the sun shines brightly in the blue sky above me. She passes through the trees and emerges into a clearing; she falls and I catch her. She rolls over facing me and is laughing. I see her smile and take off my clothes.

FLASH. I am a librarian; someone has just brought in several thousand books. I am told to sort through the first thousand, where I find a book called, *The Preacher*. It is a small black book with a companion. I seek a box full of books that look like my journal and many others.

FLASH. I am reading one of the books and discover it is a twisted pornography magazine about self-mutilation, bondage and piercing; and, they have stolen a piece of my writing and placed it within the glossy pages.

I am furious because I recognize my own hand writing. I feel violated by an unseen force, otherwise known as: Satan.

ᖗ 19 ᖕ

I leave an institution to go see a girlfriend from my past. I immediately fall in love with her again. Her blue eyes are filled with sadness and they are calling to me. She doesn't understand why I am there, and neither do I.

The institution sends people after me and I soon discover that she lives just down the street. Several of us sit at a table and we are sharing the message of Jesus, but it is hard to communicate. I want to stay with her and I almost do, but I am convinced that returning to the institution to finish my training is better. I can't undo the past. We talk about the way I used to be and I show her I am no longer the same man. I leave and return.

FLASH. I knock on her door. A child answers the door and I see several others standing behind her. I ask for the woman of the house but I don't think these children are hers. She comes to the door and the sadness is still in her eyes. I try to embrace her, but she is resistant – a man is visiting as well. I don't talk to him. I try to set her free. I can't tell her where I've come from, but I try to instill hope.

❧ 20 ☙

I am with a servant leader here on the farm when he decides to relapse, and he has chosen me as his driver. We go to the bank where he takes out a huge stack of bills, and then it is straight to the hooker stroll. He is looking for a woman, but I want a girl *and* crack cocaine.

We park the car and travel a strange route to get there; through trees and emerging underneath a bridge, where people are standing. When we arrive I see several girls. As we walk one passes by wearing only white panties and long brown hair. I take her right away. "This girl," I say. She comes willingly.

I am aroused. We slip around a corner. I press my body against hers and take her breasts in my hands. I feel her nipples hard against the palms of my hands. I am in pleasure agony and wake up.

What!? No! I can't believe this.

I go back to sleep and do it all over again; this time we go to a meeting first in the hope that he will change his mind. He doesn't and we walk out. This all continues until we end up in a room with a girl who is changing in the washroom and crack cocaine on the table.

My crack pipe falls apart and I awake again. I return to sleep and play guitar until morning.

❧ 21 ☙

Crack cocaine all night long, trying to find a girlfriend and a dealer who will deliver. I cram the white rock into my pipe, fire and inhale, but I can't get high no matter how hard I try.

❧ 22 ❧

In the first hour, I am trapped in the darkness, caught inside a dream within a dream; it is incredibly difficult to wake. At one point, I give up and say,

"Fine, speak then." I can't see anything, but I sense the presence. I lash out with my fists and connect with something. As usual, I continue to fight and awake screaming, "In the name of our Lord and Saviour Jesus Christ, I cast thee out!"

I am so captivated by the darkness that I turn on my light and lay awake for awhile, but my eyes are so tired that I can't hold them open. I turn off my light, close my eyes and fall asleep again.

❧ 23 ❧

I am transported to a house. It is suddenly filled with people, and they continue flooding in. I walk toward the nearest and cast him out of the house, saying,

"I bind you, and command you to leave." He turns, and I follow until he steps out of the threshold. Then I turn to the others and scream: "Take authority! Don't you understand what is happening!?"

I walk through the house until I find a woman; she is walking slowly, upset about what is happening. I stop her, and I find out that this is her house.

I start praying for her and telling her about Jesus. Her eyes are faded color, glossed over with white, and I know she is blind. As I am praying, her eyes begin to restore; the white leaves her eyes. I can see the iris but there is still no light.

I leave her for a moment to end the fight in the house, but when I return to her, she is once again in the darkness, whimpering the name of Jesus. I take her in my arms and heal her in the name of Jesus Christ. This time her eyes are restored completely with light burning deep inside the hazel.

I tell her that Jesus has done this for her and that he loves her.

FLASH. We are at the farm in the driving hail; I stand and start yelling,

"What are we doing!? I just healed a blind woman." As I describe what has happened I become filled with the spirit and I look around for someone to unleash the power on.

The woman stands up and comes toward me, eyes blazing; the healing is permanent. She gives me her first born daughter. I am stunned, shocked and in awe. I don't know how to process what is happening.

"Were you blind?" I ask her.

"Yes," she says.

Several people approach me, place money on the table and say, pray for me. I stand, refuse and walk away saying aloud, "You think I do this for money, but it can't be bought, it is the grace of God, and I am merely his servant."

I awake in utter ruin. God has a way of demonstrating things so that no opposition remains. Before I slept this afternoon, I said to him,

If you want to communicate with me let the vision be clear inside my mind so that I cannot forget it, otherwise let the dream fade so quickly that I can't capture it.

In response, he sends what I have just written, and it is etched into my mind.

24

I slip in and out of consciousness surrounded by strange music.

25

I take my guitar, walk out into the sand near the ocean,
and play a song to God.

David Burton

❧ 26 ❧

I dream of a beautiful girl who I meet through my sister. When we shake hands in an introduction we do not let go of each other. She also hears a *voice* that speaks to her and we have an immediate connection. I love her eyes – they are filled with light.

FLASH. She finds my notebook and writes in it, commenting on my thoughts.

❧ 27 ❧

Attacked by a demon again. I fall asleep and walk down a sidewalk where I see a cat suspended in the air. I've seen this before, I know it means a spirit is there. I run toward it and kick beneath the image into the empty air; too late I see someone to my left already captured – it is a trap. As soon as I make contact I am spun around, hands behind my back and taken captive.

"I cast you out in the name of Jesus Christ," I scream, furious and scared at the same time. I say it again and wake up yelling the words into the darkness of my room. I turn on my light and leave it on for the rest of the night.

❧ 28 ❧

Someone I know dies. I see his corpse, and there is a funeral. However, he is still alive in another body, and he looks the same. I ask him if he has a brother, trying to understand what I am seeing. I reach out and poke him with my finger to see if he is real or a ghost.

❧ 29 ❧

I travel to a far away city; it is in turmoil and the rapid transit system has been closed down, taken over and destroyed by an evil man. I walk through this man's place where he is filming a video and he tries to stop me. I say it is public land. I walk past the actors who all think the man is a slave driver and through the transit station. The buildings are torn apart, many have been made into stages for filming.

He sends two guards armed with beating sticks; I materialize two wooden swords, one for each hand, and fight with these men. I quickly disarm both of them, they flee, and I continue on my journey.

I am in search of a shelter. I find an abandoned house with many rooms. I am told by my family that I can reside in this house and no one will notice. I enter in and open the blue door. I see that the house is clean, yet barren. There are several reading chairs in the front room and a fireplace, but the house is cold: there is no fire, neither has there been for quite some time.

I brush dust off the seat of one of the chairs and place my book, open to a page, on the seat. I begin to clean the house.

✎ **30** ✎

I am laying in my bed, and I glance at my clock. It reads, ten to ten. I fall asleep, have a dream, rise and walk to the washroom. As I am walking back down the hallway, I notice my clock. It has not changed. It is the same moment, the same time.

✎ **31** ✎

I am in a military medical facility; quarantine has fallen and soldiers are sweeping room to room. In one section of the base we find an alien creature who wants to heal a member of the team.

I speak with the tongues of
men and of angels –

1 Corinthians 13:1

David Burton

CHAPTER THIRTEEN

I see a wall of flames in front of me and several dragons beyond it. A man stands beside me with weapons in both hands. The master dragon stands in the center of the flames with the others surrounding it. There is a pathway that leads directly to the creature.

The man looks at me; I ask him not to go, but he says it must be done. As I scream for him to stay, he walks straight into the fire, and approaches to the master dragon. He stands beneath its head and raises his weapons upward.

The flames begin to consume him and I watch him collapse; as he falls, the weapon in his hands goes nuclear and burns the head of the creature into non-existence.

FLASH. I enter into the house of a woman who is boring a hole into the center of a table, and sewage is spewing forth. I take the tool out of her hand and reach in with my arm, removing the blockage.

❧ 2 ❧

Something is coming, full force from the sky, an ancient evil presence. I am working in a space launch facility where the people have been deceived by Satan. A shuttle is being launched to meet this coming entity, but people start freaking out because the launch isn't authorized.

A meeting is called to discuss what is happening; I attend. Someone who is deceived stands at the front and tries to give an explanation.

"Stop," I cry out from the back of the room. I walk to the front of the room and continue speaking. "An angel, from Revelation; this is what is coming." The lights go out and the auditorium plunges into darkness.

"Pray!" I scream. "Everyone must pray." I can hear people who professed to be Christian mocking me at the back of the room and many people are fleeing.

"You pretend to be something you're not; and when the time comes, you are nothing – you are the enemy."

Several people are trying to blame me for what is happening and I step down from the stage as several guards attempt to take me into custody. I take their weapons and destroy them; when attacked, I turn it back on them and they fall beneath my movements.

A girl approaches me and says there is a way to track the shuttle, so we leave the people to their own destruction and use a lunar module to follow the shuttle's path into the atmosphere. The shuttle is destroyed as soon as it reaches a certain altitude, but the lunar module rises above and then falls back to earth, unseen by the evil that is coming.

When I return to earth, I am approached by several men who invite me to a conference, where we will discuss the fate of the earth and what can be done about it.

❦ 3 ❧

I am walking down a very dark path with a girl, through a university. I am not scared, but she is afraid. We pass through the darkness and emerge into the light, standing in front of a bookstore. We enter and she asks for directions; as we come out I turn on my flashlight to light the path.

Around the first bend of the path the moonlight is so bright that we don't need the flashlight anymore. There is a large house in the distance, and I assume that is where we are going. There are flowers on both sides of us.

"What's that smell?" she asks.

"Honeysuckles," I reply. We arrive and go to sleep, waking to someone cooking us breakfast.

❦ **4** ❧

I am in a foreign country, at war, going from village to village, searching for the enemy.

FLASH. I am back in my own country, searching for crack cocaine. I find it in a back alley; I buy some, load, fire and inhale. I go straight to a girl and kiss her, wrapping my arms around her.

She says, "No, we can't," and pulls away for a moment. Then she lifts her shirt. "Look at this," she says. I am all over her and I awake.

❦ **5** ❧

I load, fire, inhale and NOTHING.

FLASH. I am walking to an apartment that I, in times past, have used. I find it occupied, someone else has moved in. I find two keys in the hallway on the floor: one is broken, the other unlocks a nearby apartment.

I enter. At first I think the apartment is empty; however, I soon realize that there is a woman asleep on the couch underneath a blanket. She awakens and sees me, but she is not surprised or afraid, as though she has been expecting me. I tell her about the keys I have found and return them to her. I tell her I am on a mission, that I am searching for a place to watch a video, the same video that is now playing on her television.

I take this as a sign that everything is unfolding as it should. I believe this woman has a daughter and it is her daughter that I will fall in love with, a deep, soul searching love. We make a film together, a video which changes people. Years later I search for this girl again, asking to make another film to inspire the people.

FLASH. My daughter and I are standing on a bridge that we have just crossed over, and a creature is pursuing. I am a creature changed, *something I will not explain here*.

"I don't know if the power has passed to you," she screams as I turn and run toward the oncoming evil. I meet it head on in battle, and I am assured of victory. It will not touch the one I love, even if it means sacrificing my life.

I awake with these images playing across my eyes, and feelings risen within me that have no place in this mundane world.

~ **6** ~

I am in a house. An alien presence comes in and attacks me, trying to hold me down. I fight and awake screaming, "Go back to hell you piece of shit!" I shake the house with my voice.

~ **7** ~

I dream of playing guitar and singing about the cross of Jesus Christ. I have forgotten everything because I was in such a hurry this morning that I didn't write.

I run through the gateway, guitar in hand, heading for the gathering. I walk up the stairs quickly and pass through a doorway at the top. I emerge on the top of a grass covered mountainside with the ocean roaring and waves crashing at the base of the cliff. The sea is storm driven by a cold wind and a white mist hangs over the water. I am alive. I want to spread my wings and leap into the air, but I have come for a different purpose this day – the people have gathered. Before me is a choir, with a group of woman singing in the back and guitarists standing in the front.

A single woman with her long brown hair blowing in the wind leads them all. She is playing chords on her guitar, and calling them out as she plays. I can barely hear her over the wind, (A A7 Am B C Dm). I sit on the grass and add my sound to the many others; this is my reality.

"It's called ABC," a girl from the crowd behind me says. And it is over, the people disperse, some walking back through the doorway. Others, I do not know; their wings take flight, I expect.

David Burton

FLASH. I come to, wandering the streets of a distant city. The landscape is barren, buildings rise out of the dry ground. I don't know where I am supposed to go, or what I am supposed to do. I am lost. I see several people that are familiar to me, but I don't know where from. I walk with them toward a restaurant where many are meeting for dinner. When we draw closer several men from a foreign country pass by us; their conversation is strange and my attention is fixed on them.

They are talking about our clothes, how they do not fit properly [*are not right for us, are lacking: poor*]. I want to talk to them, but I don't know how to begin. I have the impression that these are important people where they come from. Finally, one man turns and addresses me. His purple shirt has what appears to be a dancing flame on it and the colors change as I watch it, the material is shimmering. I don't know if I can translate this:

"[Who are you? / What are you? / Where are you from?]"

I reply with,

"[I am a Christian / one who knows Christ / of God / harmless / lost in this world / waiting for directions.]"

It is not speech vocally as a human would understand it; impression, projection, thoughts and verbal sound are all wrapped into a single sentence. He seems pleased, almost indifferent, and he is not threatened by my presence.

"[Where are you from? What race are you? Sudan, the Middle East, Egyptian?]" I ask quickly as I turn away. He has a look of shock and surprise as he quietly turns his head without replying.

As soon as the contact is broken I am standing in front of a large gate that opens to either side, doors sliding. Guards stand beside it and several people emerge from expensive vehicles. I see the main figure climb [*crawl*] out of a white transport, but he is veiled in a black darkness. My mind refuses to see this figure, but he is aware of my gaze. I think he is shielding. I don't know why.

"He must be a prince," I say as I wake. "Of this world," I finish quietly in my mind.

⚘ 8 ⚘

I am asked by a leader to go to the inner city. I go without complaint, as I have a message to carry. He tells me I can't leave the church.

"I can't just stand here; I'm going to explode," I tell him. I open the door and walk into the courtyard, his complaints die behind me. I see a girl sitting on the curb and I join her. I think just my presence will change her, but nothing happens and I am frustrated. I stand and turn quickly, I have suddenly come alive.

"If you want to change your life, come to church tonight," I say to her – the choice is hers. I run to a wall and jump to the top of its brick facing. There is a park below where people have gathered. I tell them about God, inviting them, and then I show them who I am. The wind begins to blow as I race across the wall, leap into the sky and take flight. I balance on the wind, rising and falling, until I glide down to the grass and land.

I continue to walk the streets, but end up losing my way and find myself behind the buildings, trapped with no way out. I see a series of doors that must lead to the sunlight. I try one, expecting it to be locked, but it isn't and I run through, emerging in a corner store, out the front door and back into the sun lit street corner.

⚘ 9 ⚘

I hear the scream of jet engines, flying low to the ground, and I run outside to investigate. At first I can't see them, only hear them, but this changes as I concentrate.

"There's three of them," I say as I watch the planes quickly pass overhead. The planes are not of a standard [*human*] design: the wings are swept forward and angled. There is something very important about these planes that I need to know, and they signify something that is coming.

FLASH. I watch in horror as several people remove the intestines and vital organs from a calf while he is still alive. He walks around, struggling to hold on to life until he finally collapses near the base of a tree and dies.

FLASH. I get in an argument with my dad and leave; I travel as far as I need to until I can no longer hear his voice. I see a house and enter, walking up to a woman who can't see me. I want to have sex with her. There is another force in the room and it plays a video for me on the screen; my name is in the bottom left corner.

❧ 10 ☙

It starts in darkness; I see stars in space, and then several figures walking out of the fires of hell. I quickly realize this is demonic and close my mind.

❧ 11 ☙

I am with my mom and dad, walking through the park. We come to a steep incline and my dad starts walking upward. He stops suddenly, placing a hand on his heart. He collapses to his knees and falls to the ground. I race toward him, roll him onto his back, and I hold him close. I see his face contorted in pain and I begin to cry, placing one hand on his heart and another on his shoulder. I feel his heart pounding, racing, spasming beneath the palm of my hand. I am hurt, scared and filled with sorrow. These may be the last moments I will spend with my father.

"I love you, Dad," I whisper in his ear. I repeat it louder until he hears.

"I love you, Son." I refuse to give up.

"In the name of Jesus Christ," I begin to pray. I don't know what to pray for, I know that God can heal my dad so I ask him, as I hold him in my arms. The convulsions come in waves as I pray and then it is over.

FLASH. I have been rejected from where I was living and end up on the street. I have a backpack for my belongings and a small

Wall Between Worlds

amount of money. I feel utterly hopeless. How could this have happened again? I consider buying a tent but don't have enough money. I walk the railway tracks to another part of town. Here beside a forest path, as darkness falls, I meet a man. I try to sell him something, instead he leads me into the forest. He has several guns and talks of robbing a store. It is appealing because I am desperate, on the street with nowhere to go.

I follow him through the forest and emerge on the other side, in a parking lot of an apartment building. He climbs the steps and stands at the door. By the time I reach him another man is standing beside him, saying,

"I am in, not sure about you." I know they are talking about committing a serious crime, the man has a gun in his hand. He checks the weapon. He sees me approaching, and tells me to go wait in the forest. He will return later.

I turn and walk away. I don't want to be involved in what they are doing, it will lead straight to the depths of hell. As I cross the parking lot I see a girl being escorted by two men. She is young, black and walks in the middle of these men. I catch her eyes; she smiles, but it is empty. She is a prostitute and I know where she is going. For a moment I am envious of these men because they have a girl, wealth and a home. I have nothing and nowhere to go.

Suddenly a girl appears beside me; she is beautiful. She walks with me and talks to me. She starts talking about the bible, specifically about *Isaiah*. She tells me about the writing. I talk with her. He is a prophet, son of *Amos*, a man who lived and died a long time ago. She tells me his writing is recorded.

We stop at a picnic table and sit together. Seeing she is not wearing much, I unzip my jacket, making a movement to share my jacket with her, to keep her warm. She is surprised and motions for me to stop.

"No, keep it for yourself. You need it [*the protection*]." I have the impression that she invites me home.

David Burton

FLASH. I awaken at her house, only everything is corrupted, it is as though I have stepped into a television program. A couple of people are sitting on a couch talking. I try to interact, unsuccessfully. I walk down the hall and am attacked by a black creature crawling on all fours. It tries to attach itself to my left hand, splitting open its mouth into four segments, each with teeth and claws embedded in the skin. It attacks my hand so fast that I can't move in time. I pull my hand out of its grasp, not caring if I leave behind flesh and blood. I run to the kitchen where an old woman is standing.

"Help me," I cry out. She looks curiously at me.

"She's just hungry. She fell asleep before having her ice cream bar," she says.

"What!?"

"Your girlfriend," she says, indicating the creature following me. The old woman takes an ice cream bar and feeds it to the strange creature. As soon as the creature takes the ice cream, it bursts into a huge wave of water and a naked woman falls to the floor.

Another crest of water comes through the house, washing her away. The old woman indicates that I should follow, so I jump into the water.

FLASH. The girl and I have been together for awhile, living in the city and we are in love. She starts working at a '*knickers*' store where I visit her one day. They have television sets with provocative advertising lining the walls. She sees me watching the screens and invites me upstairs for *sevens*.

"What's that?" I ask as we walk. I find out as she removes her clothes; it means sex while at work.

FLASH. Fast forward in time. The girl and I are still in the city. The world is changing. She is offered a job at a nightclub and she is excited. I go one night to watch the performance and discover it is a nude dancing act. Several acts are strung together and I realize the managers have deceived her in cruelty.

The girl is a singer who used to win competitions, so they offered her this act. She walks out onto the stage, takes a microphone and begins to sing. The crowd that was cheering and yelling at the dancers of the previous act, go silent as she sings – then they start laughing. Finally understanding what has happened, she turns and walks away.

We leave together, trying to find a way home. We have nothing left, no money, so we ask the doorman of a hotel for change for the bus. He knows us and has known us for a long time. He is an old man, and he smiles kindly as he hands us a small brown paper bag of change. Pennies. It is not enough for both of us to get home.

"Take it," I say. "I will meet you later." Instead, we go for coffee.

FLASH. We sit across from each other, a table between us; I notice that she has a dark figure beside her, but he is obscured from direct view. It could only be one, the dark one.

"We need to pray," I say. "He is the answer; he can help us; he can provide. He is God." I close my eyes and pray. I feel filled, complete, at peace, secure and protected. I open my eyes and motion for her to pray.

She starts to pray, but she twists her words into a mockery of God and I catch on to the fact that she is making fun of the Lord. She glances at the person beside her, smiles and laughs. They conspire.

"You don't believe in God?" I ask, shocked and confused. "How is this possible? You need to turn to him and pray; otherwise your life is going to get worse." I project to her what is coming in her life, but she does not receive it.
I awake.

❧ 12 ☙

I am walking down the street in the darkness and I see a house that I know is full of evil. I stand in front and start screaming,

"I cast you out in the name of Jesus Christ!" I ask for the blood of Christ to wash this house clean and I command the demons that have taken up residence to leave. I look again and the once dark house now has light burning inside of it, spilling through the clear windows into the night.

I see a man walking toward me; as he passes me I yell:

"In the name of our Lord and Saviour Jesus Christ I cast you out! You have no authority here, no dominion! This is my earth – MY EARTH!"

FLASH. I return home to my house and talk to my wife, but I feel the presence of evil unseen around me. I express my concern to her that the demons I cast out may have followed me home. I turn on the light switch, but no light comes on. I call my wife into the bedroom. I wrap my arms around her and pull her to the bed.

"I love you."

13

"Humans can't comprehend, understand or fathom the unconditional love of God because everything in *their* life is conditional."

14

I am being held hostage in a camp outside of town. I try to escape, but there is no way. I finally get a chance to leave; I walk the driveway and try to steal a car at the parking lot near the highway. I end up catching a bus.

FLASH. I have known a girl for a long time, but she has grown up, matured, and is now seriously sexy. We return to a place where she once lived, but the people there attempt to attack her, trying to make her submit to their will.

She explodes in light, casting fireballs from her hands and pulsing white flames from her body in a circle, annihilating the people who come at her.

I pull her out of the building, telling her we must leave. We jump onto a bus and are pulling away when the police come. An officer enters the vehicle and stands beside us. He threatens me and the girl, eventually drawing his baton and striking me. I hold myself back, keeping calm and leashing my anger. The bus starts moving and the officer walks to the back. There are many people on the bus. I stand, walk to him and hurt him: I assault him brutally, and leave him for the others to finish off. I return to my seat and the driver asks if I have taken care of it. We travel across the country.

FLASH. The vehicle has changed, but I still travel through the country. I can see a map inside my mind with the ocean, several lakes and rivers marked on it. Georgia Straight is written on it, or it is spoken to me; either way I know we are heading for the sea.

I ask how we will cross this body of water because it is so far. A row boat!? No way. We arrive in the darkness and I stand on the beach among the rocks. There is no boat and the people have disappeared. I see headlights among the trees and run toward the vehicle. They are leaving me – abandoning me here.

I run after them onto the road as the daylight arrives. I reach for the girl, but she is gone. I see another girl being attacked by a man. I intercede and the man runs away. The girl is surprised and grateful; yet, we both have been deceived, hurt and abandoned. Our hands entwine and we walk away together toward the ocean.

❧ 15 ☙

I am working in a library with a woman. It is a library inside of a mansion where the books have been inherited from family members that have passed on. I think she is single, but it turns out that there is a man in her life, a man that has tortured me and physically abuses her. He tries to do it again and I realize that it will never stop.

I take him to a room beyond her view, and assault him. It is not a fight. I destroy him. He falls to the floor. I consider leaving the room, but I know this man will rise and hunt the girl again. He will inflict violence on her again, and this I can't accept. I will never allow this man to her hurt again. I take a lamp cord, wrap it around his neck, and strangle him until he is dead.

I walk out of the room and tell her that he will never hurt her again. She is concerned now that I will end up in jail and exposed. An old man is standing in the room, having arrived while I was gone.

"This is your champion; he has protected you. Love him. He needs to be shown that you love him," the old man says.

FLASH. I am in the library, searching through the books when I come across a unique, ancient text, but segments of the text and certain illustrations have been taken out. I want to know more. I seek to understand. I read the words and retain them, but they are locked away upon waking.

I open to a page that has an illustration of a wizard, with a glass ball in his hand, standing with a staff in front of him, and wind blowing the robes in the air.

"This is what I want to be," I say to someone nearby. I walk down the stairs to the front room where several people are gathered. I begin to speak when I feel a presence rise up behind me. I turn and I am faced with what appears to be a man. He is very tall, towering over me and his face is shifting shape, a blur of images.

It is Satan, or one of his creatures. We don't really talk, I just spread my arms to each side and say, "Lift me up," in expectancy. Nothing happens. It is a war of emotions with no words. I am faced with a different response: curiosity.

I want to talk but he refuses. I can't remember what happens, but he is gone as suddenly as he appears. I turn to the people gathered and start yelling,

"Did you see that!? Could you see him?"

No one saw anything; time stopped while he was present.

"We must prepare for war," I say quietly.

❧ 16 ❧

"Where do you come from?" I ask her. "Are you a dream walker like me? Or are you a program – you seem real, a person who is asleep."

She doesn't know how to answer my questions and suddenly fades away. I find someone who has destroyed a plant and I say, "You have killed her."

❧ 17 ❧

I am walking with a girl, escaping the world that seeks to destroy us. We stop and she takes off her clothes. I run my hand between her legs and she shows her sexual nature.

FLASH. I find an underground stronghold that is made with high brick walls and arched doorways: it is a disaster – no one has been here for years, but I see its potential.

❧ 18 ❧

I follow someone into a building. It looks similar to the dormitory I live in. I close my eyes, the lights go out, and I can feel the evil surround me. It grabs hold, smothering me in a blanket of darkness. I turn my head from side to side, trying to break free with my voice, but I can't. So I say the words, "In the name of Jesus Christ, I cast thee out."

I awake, screaming the words into the darkness. I catch my breath and return, this time walking down a forest path toward a building with a girl – we are talking. As we approach the final curve she starts freaking out and I take flight. She is screaming about an evil presence near the trees.

"Can't you see it!?" she screams; it is a blood curdling scream.

David Burton

"In the name of Jesus Christ, I cast thee out!"

I awake yelling the words into the night air. I catch my breath and return, this time I dream of a girlfriend I had, or will have one day. We have separated, but have come to meet each other again. When I see her I draw her close. I look into her eyes. They blaze with crystal blue light, clear and powerful: it is the most beautiful color of blue that I've ever seen and her eyes are intense.

I fall in love all over again.

❦ 19 ❧

I stand in a playground, trying to impress a girl, but my mom picks me up and drives me up a mountain. I age in the vehicle, changing from a child to a man. My mom drives recklessly on the snow covered roads. I am scared and become angry.

"I hate these vehicles," I say. "Especially in winter. I keep thinking we are going to slip on the ice and drive over a cliff."

She slows down as we arrive at the top of the mountain. It is a space launch facility, called *Helifinity* or something similar. It is Satan's creation, designed to keep people ignorant of the truth. There is an office building in the front and a laboratory in the back. A set of steps descends to the lab and prostitutes are standing in a line, talking to a nurse. These woman are paid to give blood. There is a symbol on several shipping containers and everything seems all too familiar. I need to get closer to investigate, so I leave the vehicle and attempt to infiltrate a restaurant where the employees of this place go for pleasure, entertainment and dining.

I take several people with me; we are a resistance of a sort, and we are dressed as people of wealth, knowing this is acceptable and will not draw attention to ourselves.

My mom is taken captive while we are in the building, but she leaves several letters written in her own hand, so that we will know the truth. I read the letter, but have forgotten its contents; and one remains unopened. We are exposed. I have lost what comes next: a firefight, and many soldiers.

FLASH. I am in a house where someone is trying to communicate with me. I find a hidden room, filled with old photographs, books and clothes. It is the computer system that I search for this night, because I know it holds the information I need, but I awake before I find it.

⟡ 20 ⟡

I am in the night air, palms down, hovering in the sky. I am on a hillside in front of the ocean; another time I am on a grass covered lawn of a house.

The specifics of this dream don't really matter, I believe. Someone was trying to control my life, so I spread my wings and flew away: the message is clear.

⟡ 21 ⟡

The first attack comes as some as I close my eyes. I awake instantly, saying, "In the name of Jesus." And then I stop. At the name alone, it is over. I return to sleep and start dreaming of the girls.

At first, two girls are with me, tempting me. I travel with them to a place outside of town. I want to have sex, but they do not. They only want to tease.

FLASH. "Because I know more about this than you do."

⟡ 22 ⟡

I find a series of blank cheques, already signed; I return them to the owner for a reward. He decides to give me a handful of crack cocaine. I want money, but he hands me white rock instead. I demand his pipe; load, fire and inhale.

For the first time since I started smoking crack ten years ago, I actually get high in my dream. I try to repeat the process

David Burton

immediately, but in my vision the rock melts into a pool of liquid and the liquid swirls down, emptying into a basin.

I inhale until it is gone; I do this several times. I still have a handful of rocks and many in my mouth. I walk up to the man [*Satan*] and spit the rocks in his face, throw my burning hot pipe into his hand, and cast my rocks away.

I turn and leave, *waking up*.

23

I am running across a grass covered plain, carrying two swords in my belt. I come to a wall made of stone bricks; I remove one to hide my weapons behind it.

A tidal wave comes and washes away the world. A girl I love is in the water so I run to her and hold her in my arms, as we flow with the flood. We are in distress, but we have each other in the storm.

24

God comes to have a conversation which I have forgotten and then several of us come together to pray; it gets right out of hand quite quickly. I manifest some other language in another voice as I stand and throw my bible at someone. Then the spell breaks and I am free.

I see evil fall upon a man and pass from him; it is pulled away as a cloud. I go from person to person, screaming,

"Show me your eyes!"

Until the evil is gone, it is war.

David Burton

For I know the things that
come into your mind, every
one of them.

Ezekiel 11:5

David Burton

CHAPTER FOURTEEN

I walk from world to world, from dream to dream, passing through portals and watching the landscape change around me. I walk through the portal, the sky darkens, thunder and lightning come and then the world shifts.

I awake utterly exhausted.

❧ 2 ❧

I am working in a grocery store; a girl bends over to clean out the bottom of a display case. She is singing, "Be my lifelong passion, Jesus." Her voice and appearance are beautiful. I want to wrap my arms around her, but instead I walk away out of sight, raise my hands and start singing as well.

I realize I don't belong here and start drinking. I walk away from the work, but before I leave the store I place the bottle on the counter.

As I walk outside I see the world is in literal darkness; I run, spread my wings and fly, screaming out scripture at the top of my lungs. I stay in the air until I awake.

❧ 3 ❧

I am at the academy and we are attacked by witchcraft. I walk quickly down the hall to the children's class and speak to them about Jesus. I try to explain who he is and why we need to pray to him. I don't know how successful I am, but my voice is filled with passion. As I turn to leave, I discover that a demon has entered the building, but two of us isolate him in a room and kill him. As he dies his body turns into insects that scurry out from beneath his corpse, climbing the walls. I've seen this before, but usually they just disappear; these insects go on the attack.

I walk out onto a balcony and close the glass sliding door behind me.

❧ 4 ❧

I am in the water, swimming in a lake, and something is pulling me deeper. I look beneath my feet, see the edge approaching, and the darkness of the abyss below. I wave my hands, pushing myself away from the dark. I sense the presence of something down there, waiting to rise up and drag me below.

❧ 5 ❧

A funeral in the mountains; snow covers the ground in a white blanket for as far as the eye can see. A woman is walking through the snow toward a small house; I follow and listen to the conversation. She is asking about a funeral; a man answers that it is being held right now.

She wants to know why she was not informed (she lives separate from the rest); he says it involves another clan, many were flown in. Old wounds and arguments, bad blood that they do not want to resurface, and only these two old ones remember the cause of the conflict.

❧ 6 ❧

"You are not translating properly; the word is not *safe* it is *alien*." I turn to find the darkness has come; all the lights are off.

❧ 7 ❧

I find a house powered by nuclear energy and a missile bomb in the ocean, near the shore in shallow water. It has a handle on it, which I take hold of.

❧ 8 ❧

I enter a house, dressed as a servant to hide my presence. I walk through the doorways and out into the garden. As I am looking at the flowers I see a girl drowning in the pool.

I run to the edge of the water, removing my clothes as I close the distance, and dive perfectly into the water. I take the girl in my arms, holding her close, and force air into her lungs.

She returns to the land of the living.

FLASH.

I am still near the pool when a man enters the courtyard and attacks me, verbally at first; physically shortly afterward.

He wants the book I am reading. I tell him it is not mine to give, that he must ask the girl. I tell him that if he wants a book, go to the library.

He comes running at me intent on violence; I stand and strike him in the forehead with my fist. He flies thirty feet and falls on the ground. I leap into the sky and land on top of him, pressing my hand on his chest.

"Do not rise," I say. I start crying as I speak because my eyes are opened to the truth: he is a decrepit, frail, wasting away shadow of a person, who Satan holds in bondage. His skin is sunken and shriveled, he is withered.

I start witnessing to him as tears fall from my eyes. I tell him about repentance, asking Jesus to enter, power and grace; I tell him he can't earn it, nothing he can do will ever be enough. It is a gift from God, freely given – he just has to accept it.

He stands and I search his eyes for light; there is a spark, but it is far distant. His face has already changed and I know there is hope. I tell him to pray, and I awake.

❦ 9 ❧

I have a dream about pornography that eliminates all other dreams from memory. I am with a girl who tells me that it is wrong and she is very upset; she has found magazines in my room. She tries to make a point by bringing a bunch of girls to my house who all agree that it is wrong and have reasons why.

My girlfriend disappears. When I enter my room I find all the magazines have been opened and lay scattered around my room, open to various photographs. I am shocked. I know she has been here, but she is gone.

This is a test. I close all the magazines, gather them together and throw them into the trash can. It is only then that I see light coming from the closet. I walk over and find her, she has fallen asleep.

10

I am standing beside the ocean and schools of fish are splashing through the water near the shore, in the shallows. I walk closer to see why these fish are jumping, and I see something rise out of the water, a humpback whale.

I walk up a flight of stairs behind me to see the creature from a clearer angle. I see its huge body beneath the surface of the water. A girl stands beside me. I take her in my arms and kiss her. We stand in the sun with the seaside before us.

11

She sees me leaving and comes in my room.

"Why are you leaving?" she asks, filled with the spirit. "I come here to listen and talk with you every night," she says. I remember her laying on the bed with me, her hands on my arm, looking at me intently.
The depth of connection I have with this girl is beyond the earthly realm; we have known each other forever. I wrap my arms around her and pull her onto my lap. I stare into her eyes. She is the only one.

"Who are you?" I awake saying. "Who are you?"

12

I am standing in a room, looking a map of north America. On the map the boundaries of the countries have changed; Canada remains

David Burton

divided into the same provinces, but the states have fallen and new boundaries have been established. Foreign nations rule these new territories. I am watching one of these territories in the center of the land expand, and for some reason I am concerned.

⁓ 13 ⁓

I run, breaking through the barrier and leap into the sky. I am descending in the air over a flight of steps. I free fall, arms extended to each side. They have tried to stop me, but I refuse to listen. I see a soldier ascending the steps.

I land in front of him and throw him to the ground when he tries to stop me. I run and leap into the air again.

FLASH. I return to the barracks of a military base where people are very angry with me – they say I am rebellion. I tell them they do not understand. They take away my room and I am given a hard mattress on the floor.

I awaken in the night and dress in the army fatigue that has been left for me. I can hear people shouting in the distance in a strange language. I stand and see soldiers running from all directions toward the sound, near an airfield. I follow.

A girl tries to lead me through the chaos; she is leading my group. I recognize someone I know so I stop, remove my gloves and shake his hand.
"I made that jump," I say.

"I know you did," he replies.

I enter a building and walk through several sections; each section has soldiers with creatures chained to them. Some come near me, but I withdraw.

When we reach our destination we embrace, the girl and I – then all hell breaks loose. I feel a reaction on my skin. I look down and see a rash starting on my arms; it is red and rough texture, spreading in linear patches. I freak out.

"What have you done to me!?" I scream.

"You're having an allergic reaction," she says.

Like hell I am; the disease spreads like fire, I can feel sores appearing on my face and all over my body. I can see it flowering and growing like fungus all over me. I run my hands over my face, wanting to tear it off, but afraid that my flesh will come with it.

I start screaming: JESUS, over and over again. I scream for him to forgive my sins. I list them, but can't remember them. I am desperate, screaming and burning from the sores.
I find a dirty pane of glass and I stare into it. I see my physical face with blue eyes looking sad, staring out from the foggy mirror. I know that this has somehow been cast upon me, it is a lie no matter how real it seems.

I cry out to Jesus and he frees me. I don't know how. In the blink of an eye, I am changed, restored and angry. I leap into the air with renewed strength, in a fury, breaking through glass windows all around me, searching for my enemy.

I find myself in a garden with creatures that attempt to stay out of my reach, but can't. I'm fast, I have learned, and right now, I am furious.

FLASH. I awake in my bed; there is a briefcase beside it. I open the case, finding a black jump suit.

"You've been assigned to [*place*]. You will be free falling 25,000 feet."

I am excited, the other people are confused and nervous.

"Would you like to see my technique?" I ask laughing.

☜ 14 ☞

I am riding up the street toward home. There are trees ahead of me and houses on either side of the street. A ball of fire, flashing with light, passes overhead and crashes in the distance, over the mountains.

I stop dead in my tracks and stand still, my eyes turn toward the crash site. I watch in silence as the clouds are pulled inward; storm clouds, black and white, rolling quickly: compressing behind the mountain.

The sky is empty for a moment and then there is an explosion that rocks the world. At first, I think it is a nuclear weapon. A huge ball of darkness appears near the mountain; it pulses waves of dark fire, upward.

I look to my left and see a young girl standing in the doorway of her house. I run up the pathway and enter the house with her. I take her in my arms and pull her back from the world. I fear the atmosphere has been contaminated or destroyed. We close the door and look out the front window.

I see the plant life turn into a black oily substance and melt, oozing into the ground. I am scared. Soon, we witness an army of soldiers encased in machines, a mechanical suit of battle armour: they are destroying the houses around us, tearing them to pieces.

I begin to wonder why these men have joined the enemy; then I wonder if they are even human at all. Our house will be next – I open the door and flee, hoping to outrun the destruction and find a safe haven; but, I fear there is no place left on earth to find.

❦ 15 ❦

"I have had a vision," I say.

Certain people will attempt to cease control, but the creation must remain in my hands or it will fail.

David Burton

The diseased have ye not
strengthened, neither have ye
healed that which was sick,
neither have ye bound up that
which was broken, neither
have ye brought again that
which was driven away, neither
have ye sought that which was
lost; but with force and with
cruelty have ye ruled them.

Ezekiel 34:4

David Burton

CHAPTER FIFTEEN

I am made of *light*, and lifted into the sky, soaring upward around a huge storm, white cloud with lightning flashing around the outside. I see the earth far beneath me.

2

I am attacked as soon as I close my eyes; demons come and I cast them out in the name of Jesus Christ. I return to sleep and stand near a river. I walk into the water until it is at about my knees, and I understand that this is the water of God.

I am transferred back to my room, standing in the darkness as demons encircle me, tormenting. I fight but can't wake. My spirit refuses to enter my body and rise, so I hold on with all the strength I have.

This happens several times in a row, until the last time that I stand in the water, and I realize that by passing through the river I am doing something I don't understand and sending myself into the trap.

"DON'T DRINK THE WATER!" I scream and snap wide awake.

3

The world [*earth*] is dying and several people are escaping the destruction. I am one of them. We rise in a ship to the sky, into the darkness of space. I am hidden among the people and no one knows who I am. It remains that way for a long time until I begin to reveal myself. Then the people become angry with me because of what I am, and because of the power I have.

FLASH. I search through the wreckage of a broken world.

꙰ **4** ꙰

I am crossing the land around a mountain, alongside the ocean; a hurricane comes and floods the pathway: the storm is incredible.

An eagle picks me up from the ground and flies me toward my destination. I see the destruction that has begun and the wind is so strong that we can't pass.

"Fly above the clouds," I say to the eagle.

We rise up through the gray storm clouds and emerge on top of the world. A circular platform of cloud spirals outward from a sphere in the center. In the sphere there is a set of stairs that lead to a doorway. I know this door is important, but I don't have access to it at the moment. I have the impression that we will fly the distance required to pass over the storm.

The eagle explains something completely different. He begins to speak of time travel. He says that we will fly around the sphere for several rotations and then descend back to the same place on earth, time will have passed, but I don't understand how. He mentions the moon as part of this, it's the name of the process.

I am placed standing on the clouds. I find it a firm surface beneath my feet, and I start walking immediately toward the doorway, I am drawn to it. The eagle picks me up; he says I am not to open this door. We fly around the sphere and just before we descend I see a trail of footprints left in the wisp of cloud near the stairway.

This place has no wind; the air is still.

We fall into the open sky below where the sun is shining brightly. I am shocked. Although we spent only minutes above the cloud, hours, if not days, have passed on earth.

I stand in awe of the destruction that has been wreaked upon the land near the ocean; everything is gone and even the sand itself has been in a great upheaval. There is a crying rising into the air from the earth. I think the eagle and I are the only ones who hear.

David Burton

❧ **5** ❧

We are walking along the ocean, the sand of the beach beneath us stretches out into the waves pounding the shore. I know this place; she sees a building in the distance and wants to enter it.

"Why?" I ask her, she doesn't have a reason except that there is a fear within her about being in the open. I come to the open doors at the far end, and the ocean beyond.

"I suppose we could pass through," I say silently. As soon as we enter we are in each other's arms.

❧ **6** ❧

I dream of a coven, splitting into two groups, not going to war with each other but having a difference of opinion: one side is hiding from the other.

FLASH. Two women are walking toward my friend. They are both sexy, but he only loves one of them. When I have a moment I walk to the girl and speak with her. I could destroy her, instead I warn her.

"Do not hurt him; he is my friend." I turn and walk away.

❧ **7** ❧

I walk through a doorway and several dark figures, whose faces are indistinguishable, surround me. They know who I am. They are led by a girl, who approaches me and says,

"We are watching you." I feel her support, not the condemnation I expected.

❧ **7** ❧

I am in space far above the earth, trying to secure something to something else; I fear that someone may be hurt. In the blink of an eye I am returned to the earth and I find myself walking down a long road in the rain. I am approaching the plateau and just as I crest the mountain I see clearly an Island and water to one side, a city to the other. The rain is pouring, soaking my clothes, so I decide to descend into the valley and seek refuge.

What I find is evil. All I want to do is leave the city, travel to my homeland, and find a way out. While in this city I become involved with a woman who has a child. I attempt to build trust with the child, but the child is no longer human. I find the child hiding in a dark place, and I coax it out into the light.

There is a part of me that experiences revulsion at this contact with the creature; it has human form, and it can speak at a high level, but it seems completely alien to me. I come to find myself attached to this child in many ways, but I must leave.

I ask anyone, and everyone, I can until someone offers me a lift out of town.

✿ 9 ✿

The girl with black hair; we are supposed to be together but there is a wall between us, something keeping us separated. I see her and speak to her for a moment before the wall comes crashing down. I search for another way.

FLASH. I stand on the grass near a school. I see a few people gathered together. As I walk toward them I see a youth holding a bag of marijuana, showing his friends. I think he is about to sell some of it.

I know it means slavery for all of them, so I walk up to him, and snatch it out of his hands even though he doesn't want to let go. I tell him not to use this drug because it will destroy his life and everything it touches. I express the danger and confront him.

"Look around," I say. "This is a school, look at the children. You can't sell here, and if you do I will kill you." I am trying to express the seriousness of the matter, because he has been raised to think of marijuana as a small thing which causes harm to no one, but his soul knows it is a lie. As he begins to grasp the clarity of the situation, evil comes for him to take it away.

I take his jacket in my fists and lift him off the ground; he is before me, suspended in the air.

"Leave," I say. "Do it away from here." I am angry. I throw the plastic bag filled with marijuana at him and walk away. A man is walking quickly toward me, asking what I am doing.

He says he knows all about what is happening with the youth and it is just fine by him, and the world standard. I freak out and push him to the ground.

"You know and you do nothing!?" I am enraged. I lean over and pick the man up off the ground. I place him on his feet, turn and walk away: these people know nothing.

10

I am in a school, moving from classroom to classroom. I feel alive, complete and free. I walk outside for a break and sit at a table with several people. A beautiful girl sits next to me. I talk to her and share my heart with her, but the man on the opposite side of the table attempts to lie to her about me, and condemns her. I show her love and acceptance, embracing her.

FLASH. I am at the school but in a different area. I walk through the dining hall and pass through a doorway into a hidden room. There are musical instruments hanging on the walls. I select a guitar and start playing. I sing a song about a flash of blue white light and the coming of something powerful. I can't remember the words, but I feel at peace and a joy rising in my spirit. Someone in the distance closes the door and I hear a piano being played behind it.

11

I am in a room filled with people, attached to a church sanctuary. There is a doorway at the far end of the room which people are coming out of. They walk into this room and say a message, speaking into a microphone.

They all talk of God, but know nothing about him. They pass all sorts of nonsense off as divine revelation. I can't stand it anymore – words are burning inside of me. I take the microphone and begin speaking. I am raging but speaking clearly: you do not understand or have the power of God, is the basis of my speech.

I am walking around the room with a microphone until a man enters the room who has obviously been sent by the church to silence me.

"I am being thrown out for telling you the truth," I say. I am escorted out of the room, through the front entrance of the church, and as I cross the foyer I am given a vision of a man wrapping a microphone cord into a ball, throwing it at the front doors of the church and walking out.

"This is how the church will split," I say aloud as I walk outside. Several men in suits emerge from the church and approach me. There is an evil presence that is hoping for me to be hurt, but instead one of them calls me by name and asks me to follow him.

We enter the church and walk down the hallway to a room; it has a desk, several candles lining the walls and a door. There is a man behind the desk. I am unsure of what to expect. I sit down and he begins talking about scripture. He is asking me what I think.

I am unaware of the sequence of the next events, but I will write what I know. Someone is accusing me and this man defends me, saying,
"I have been following this man for several years as he is becoming a monk. I have been watching him from a distance, and reading his work."

He says something that leads me to approach his desk and pick up a book that lay there.

"It sounds like you have been reading something you shouldn't." I say. I flip through the pages and recognize my own material, but much of it is missing – this man has only fragments.

One piece is titled **GATEWAY**; it is a divided section that stands alone. The other section contains writing of God and the angels. I see a drawing of wings on one of the pages. I am interested. I return the book and sit down.

"Why have you asked me here?"

"I heard you speaking and came as quickly as I could." He hands me a list of questions that he wants to discuss. I remember two of them. The first is *quick recovery* and the second is, *power of the air*. These are the first and last questions on the list. The rest of the list is obscured from my vision, and I can't read it.

I read the first question and answer: "No," quickly; "It will take a very long time," but then I change my mind while reasoning.

"Experiencing God's power, or presence, is the only way," I reply. "Perhaps this could change someone quickly because once this event occurs they will never be the same again."

This is the general concept, but I am missing words. I see the question but I do not have a chance to answer it because we are disrupted by something trying to enter the room and the connection is broken.

12

I walk toward a storm, drawn to it because I know I will find something there in the raw power of God displayed in the sea. Waves crash against the shore and the streets are flooded with water.

Someone tries to force me away from the storm, but I kick and scream until I am free. I run to the water's edge through a series of hallways and doors.

230

David Burton

Every man's work shall be
made manifest: for the day
shall declare it, because it shall
be revealed by fire; and the fire
shall try every man's work of
what sort it is.

1 Corinthians 3:13

David Burton

CHAPTER SIXTEEN

I am working as a cook in a restaurant, but being treated as a slave; being commanded to do disturbing things, corrupt and unclear. The person who has employed me, the person who owns the restaurant is standing beside me, asking me to do something with several creatures laying on the grill.

I refuse. I can sense the evil within this man and more importantly I understand that he considers me nothing. He is trying to enforce this upon me, that I am a slave and worthless. I am neither, and I am finished with allowing people to keep me captive or oppressed.

I walk away from the man, take off my apron and exit the building. I walk into the parking lot, step onto the hood of a vehicle and start jumping up and down, crushing the metal beneath my feet.

I walk from vehicle to vehicle, destroying them. I see a small set of stairs leading toward a door, and I know the restaurant lay behind that door. As I approach, I look for a weapon. I see a rake; it seems appropriate. I gather it in my hand and ascend the steps in a single motion.

I pass through the doorway and my eyes are assaulted with the image of a dining hall. The tables are covered in white cloth and set with silver cutlery, sparkling wineglasses intersperse the settings. I see money sitting on small black platters, but everything I see is a forgery.

This entire restaurant is a lie; this is the window dressing that hides the evil from its patrons. My eyes see the truth, and the slavery behind it. I take my rake and draw it across the table, sending cutlery, glasses and cash flying into the air.
As I hear the objects crashing to the floor I leap onto the table and continue to work my way across the room; my decision is made: I have become resolute.

At the far end of the hall a boy is dining with his family. As I sweep away the lies set before him, he is offended. He looks at me with disgust and anger. He is indignant and he begins to speak – I stop him quickly with my reply. My eyes are on fire as I speak,

"If you consider this an injustice, look at *my* life." I have silenced the child, and I have stayed long enough.

❧ 2 ☙

I am standing in the grass near a building here on the farm. I am speaking another language: I start quietly and increase volume as I form the words. I spread my hands to each side and I feel the power surging all around me; it flows into me through my outstretched hands: I can't see the world around me anymore.

Suddenly the power manifests as two blazing white wings directly in front of me, lightning dancing around them. I am aware of what is happening. I know I am about to return to the physical world. I place my hands in front of me, opening and closing my fingers as everything around me passes into darkness.

My hands flash with opalescent color until I am here. I awake, opening my eyes, and rising in the dawn's early light.

❧ 3 ☙

I awake in the air, in flight. I approach a house where everyone expects that I will land and walk among the people. Instead I rise higher, soaring above their heads and entering the building from a balcony. I touch down for a moment, take a few steps and leap skyward again. I crash through panes of glass that were probably windows and fly over a large dining hall. The tables are covered in white cloth.

As I reach the edge of the next opening, I cling to the ledge as my flight fails me for a moment; I am caught unaware, but only for a single moment.
I pull myself to the ledge, run several steps and take flight, crashing through another set of window panes. I reach the final balcony on the far end of the house. I stand for a moment, quietly looking out

over the grass lawn, wooden fence and dull glowing streetlights before stepping off the railing and gliding on the air.

FLASH. I am in a barn with a demon and the animals; at first I think nothing of this demon, when suddenly Satan comes within him. I watch as the horns grow up out of the pasty skin and then wrap around the back of his head. The evil is increasing; the demon is changing. At next glance he is fully aroused and he starts fucking the animals. I am disgusted and horrified. I don't think this demon is aware of my presence. I walk around him and leave the barn.

FLASH. I am in a room, dimly lit. There is a single table in the center of the room with two chairs on either side. There is a metallic ball in the center of the table and I sit in one chair, facing another person. We awake at the same moment, somewhat disoriented: neither of us know why we are here or what is happening.

The sphere in the center of the table has slots carved into it and from these cuts a red light begins to glow. As the light gets brighter it shifts through the spectrum, ending in a brilliant white light that I raise my hands to shield my eyes from.

The other person is terrified, even as I am fascinated.

"It is taking us somewhere," I say. I feel the shift, but it is quick, and without disorientation. I stand and examine my surroundings.
I am in another room, as empty as the first; however, there are two openings on either side of the room – doorways. I walk to the doorway and look through. There is a large empty area brightly lit with white light. It appears to be a large enclosed room, designed for practice or testing.

I see several objects, and I understand, but don't simultaneously. I turn and walk to the other doorway; peering through, I see the same area of containment, with several differences in the objects. The wall to my left is embedded with equipment and covered in strange symbols. I inherently know that this is a testing ground.

I blink only to find myself standing in the center of the room I was just looking at, as creatures materialize out of nowhere and attack

Wall Between Worlds

immediately. I am surprised more than anything else. One creature attaches itself to my back. I pull, trying to remove the protective clothing I am wearing.

I toss it to one side, and I awake.

～❦ **4** ❦～

I dream of her. I love her without fail, as she has given me a chance. We stand in a room, lined with glass windows, with the ocean beyond the glass – speaking in quiet tones.

We leave and walk across the grass near the ocean.

"All of this is mine," I say. I feel complete and confident in myself. I speak truth. When evil comes to separate us, I say, "I'll take care of this."

I enter the battle and end the attack.

～❦ **5** ❦～

Flight training. I am teaching a young girl how to lift, fly and glide – hands extended to each side, palms down.
FLASH. I am walking outside of a building where many of us have gathered. There is a discussion going on which I am interested in. I have forgotten it entirely.

As I look away from the gathering my gaze falls on the sky across the field: there is a doorway etched in the clouds. All else fades away.

"Look," I cry out. "There is a doorway in the clouds." As others begin to turn their attention to what is happening, I am already scanning the horizon; several openings are appearing. When the number reaches three I spring into action. I will not be caught in stasis again.

I start running across the field toward a doorway; the doorway is a doorframe opening in the clouds, the base of each pillar touches the earth, within the opening I can see another world with the sun shining brightly. It appears as the image I have drawn except that it is open in a white wall of cloud.

The opening is massive. I can see it clearly in the distance. I know that I will not reach it in time before it closes. I reach out with arms extended to each side and draw power into me. I hold it inside, reach forward with my hands and hurl a pulse of power toward the opening.

As it reaches the gateway, I explode it outward in an air concussion. (There is more to this, but I can't explain. I am doing what I can't remember.) The gateway is expanded in either direction, but continues to close. Now I begin to sense a presence from the other side, somehow we have allowed ourselves to be known.

I run further, and as I run I repeat the process, extending my hands: outstretched arms, palms out. I have drawn the power within me, and hold it inside – I hear my own voice of thought:

"*Draw, hold, release.*"
The third time I allow the power to flow through me something different happens. I see the silver white lightning ball of power soaring from my fingertips. I am seeing a different dimensional perception. The first two times I could not see, only sense and know what I was doing. On this one I was concentrating on the release more than the draw: I watch it pass through the doorway.

As it begins to crest and arc skyward, I throw a pulse [*of sound*] with my hand and it explodes in a fury: uh, oh. I had become caught up in what I was doing as I ran across the field. Each time I pushed myself to draw deeper on the power and held it [*differently: changed, shaped it somehow*], until I had created the shimmering gray translucent ball.

For a moment, nothing happens; and suddenly the explosion renders in the physical realm. Trees are uprooted and tossed in the air, a dark cloud of storm driven wind swirls and the gateway collapses.

I sense the presence on the other side of the opening as it is collapsing into the chaos I have cast. He is angry and in a last dying gesture he throws a tree at me. I stop running and stand watching the awesome destruction I have somewhat accidently caused. A tree is coming straight for my path, flying horizontally.

I launch myself into the air, land on its wide trunk and ride it backwards to where it lands. I casually jump to the ground and calmly walk toward the people I left.

"I hope that this answers that particular question."

৵ **6** ৵

A starship has been built and it is keyed to the pilot's genetic code: the engines will not fire without the pilot. The ship will remain dormant without the pilot. I have fought for a very long time to see this starship get off the ground and into the sky.

৵ **7** ৵

I am in a building made of stone, looking out over an ocean; I am talking with someone. I find words tattooed around my groin and inner thigh. The words are a message that I have left for myself.

The final section of text has to be held to a mirror so that the words can be read. I am a prophet. In my hands is a drawing of mechanical armour, a suit technology, and of a chamber in the earth with something leading skyward.

I have seen these images before. I remember creating them long ago. Where have they been? All of this has remained hidden so that the enemy can have no chance of taking the knowledge before my time comes.

As I look out over the ocean I sense a pulse of energy in the distance, and the ocean begins to recede. I move quickly into action, running for the pathway that has been exposed beneath the sea.

I watch the water pouring into a large hole that was hidden under the sea; in the distance a tidal wave is racing toward shore. I run down the path, moving quickly to the opening in the ground. The wave is directly in front of me, and the hole is empty.

Yet I know this is where I left it. I reach the edge and jump into the air. I land on an invisible object, the ship, and I am transported to freedom.

The starship reacts with my body; my flesh and its armour become one; I feel an increase of strength. The changes happens fast and I watch my muscle structure alter, becoming the suit technology.

When the change is nearly complete I am drawn into a confrontation; I react with no fear and renewed strength, almost annihilating the accuser.

$\sim$ **8** $\sim$

We are called, chosen; the time arrives when black clothing is given each of us: we stand on opposing sides of a sea of water, each on a mountain.

I am preparing for flight, and rows of explosives line the gate from which I will launch myself.

FLASH.

I stand on a mountain, dressed in white; I am here, about to [*ascend; descend*] in flight to carry the message of God – I spread my wings and launch myself from the mountain.

The message is in two parts; I become both the segments of the message: the first upon the mountain, and the second upon the ground.

I awake with my eyes, tired.

$\sim$ **9** $\sim$

I just watched the world burn, unless it was the fires of hell I have seen. I am standing outside of a building; cars have been tossed around and crushed, the sky is black.

The light of fires burning all around me flickers in the darkness; the world is destroyed. I walk up the road to a platform. I see several sets of stairs leading upward inside of a building.

This is where I want to go, but I can't because there is a chain link fence surrounding the courtyard where the stairway begins. I turn and look out over the valley; fires burn all across the city, enveloping streets and spreading outward from the center: a mountain nearby is also consumed in flames.

I see several vehicles passing, seeking a way out of the horror. I look into the sky: a platform is extended from the dark cloud and a chain hangs from it.

I reach my hand upward and call the chain; it comes falling to earth in response to my call.

And the angel that talked with
me came again, and waked me,
as a man that is wakened out
of his sleep.

Zechariah 4:1

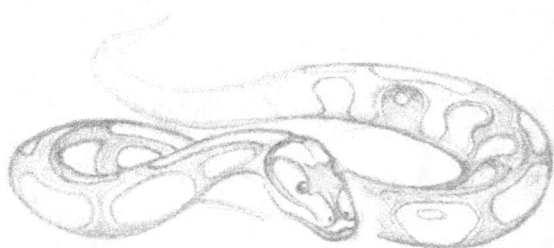

David Burton

EPILOGUE

I am in darkness being tormented by a demon; crack cocaine is everywhere and I am being held prisoner. He threatens me with violence; I try to appease him, but nothing works – he is intent on destroying me. I try to escape, but he blocks every door.

FLASH.

I am upstairs with crack cocaine in my hand. I enter a room and try to lock the door behind me so that I can use in peace. I discover that the handle does not lock and the deadbolt is broken: the door has been kicked in and the frame is broken. I desperately want to get high and be alone with my tiny electric light and naked girls.

FLASH.

I am downtown in a restaurant, trying to make a phone call to my dad. The line is disconnected in the middle of our conversation. A woman's voice fills the empty space of the phone line.

"Calls can't be made after a certain time."

I turn and walk to the glass window, digging in my pockets for spare change. I pull out a quarter, as another hits the floor and rolls away. I ask to use the phone; the woman at the window says wind knocked a tree onto the line.

At the same moment that I explain I need to call for a ride, I hear my name being called from the dining room. It is my father's voice, and I run to him. I didn't think he would come.

We exit the building, but as we exit I choose the wrong shoes. I find my own and we walk out; the night is cold, snow is everywhere and ice holds the earth in its grip. As we walk toward the front path we see many people, all dressed in regular clothes, smiling and going to church. Everything appears normal; nothing is amiss except the clouds of white smoke pouring from the automobiles.

"Not that way," he says, and turns to walk around behind the building. I jump over the snow bank, feeling playful and happy that we are together.

FLASH.

We are walking down a city street; buildings touch the sky all around us: it is deserted – not a soul walks these streets, not a single vehicle.

We walk in a straight line in the center of a narrow street, heading toward a tower directly ahead. I look up into the blue sky at the top of the tower and my vision becomes crystal clear, burning into my mind.

A rainbow shines in an arc over the pinnacle of the tower, a sun rises from behind the tower and a second arc of rainbow light spectrum intersects the first.

I am spun in a circle, twice; and when I look again, the world has returned to a dull faded light that now appears dark in comparison to the light I have just witnessed. I grab hold of my dad, burying my head in his shoulder, crying:

"Why did I look away?" It is a soul retching cry of sheer agony, desperation and loss.

I turn to look at the tower again and the crystal clarity returns; the sky is blue, a single arc of rainbow shines across the pinnacle, but a figure of sheer darkness stands small in front of the light.

My mind cannot pierce the darkness; it ascends and descends in a red flame. I start speaking of Jesus, saying what little I know of him, mistaking this figure for something it is not. I am panicking; nothing is making sense. I try to look away, as the figure is aware of me – my vision telescopes and I see the figure closer. I am freaking out, becoming filled with fear.

I try to move, but my dad holds me bound; he will not allow me to turn and look away. He pushes me closer and the tower disappears: I am staring at a concrete wall with a faded drawing of wings etched in white paint. The world has grown dull again; the light faded: still I grasp at understanding.

I look at my dad; he still holds me immobile and his face is turned to the side, head down with a look of utter sadness upon his face. Sorrow for which the depth is unknown, but great; it pains me to see him this way.

"Jesus," I say. And then it dawns upon me. I hold on to him with all my strength and whisper to him,

"My Father."

The world immediately and completely changes: the light has returned, the world, even the air, feels alive. We are holding each other, walking down the street; and, he is smiling as if nothing ever happened.

I AWAKE.

FINISH

David Burton

Arise, shine; for thy light is
come, and the glory of the
LORD is risen upon thee.

Isaiah 60:1

www.ingramcontent.com/pod-product-compliance
Lightning Source LLC
LaVergne TN
LVHW051114080426
835510LV00018B/2031